Splash of Color

A Rainbow of Brilliant Black-and-White Quilts

Jackie Kunkel

Martingale®
Create with Confidence

Dedication

To my better half and husband, Rod;
my fantastic children, Adrianne and Brian;
and Mom and Dad.

Martingale®
19021 120th Ave. NE, Ste. 102
Bothell, WA 98011-9511 USA
ShopMartingale.com

Printed in China
20 19 18 17 16 15   8 7 6 5 4 3 2 1

Library of Congress Cataloging-in-Publication Data is available upon request.

ISBN: 978-1-60468-605-0

Mission Statement

Dedicated to providing quality products and service to inspire creativity.

Credits

PUBLISHER AND CHIEF VISIONARY OFFICER
Jennifer Erbe Keltner

EDITORIAL DIRECTOR
Karen Costello Soltys

DESIGN DIRECTOR
Paula Schlosser

MANAGING EDITOR
Tina Cook

PHOTOGRAPHER
Brent Kane

ACQUISITIONS EDITOR
Karen M. Burns

PRODUCTION MANAGER
Regina Girard

TECHNICAL EDITOR
Nancy Mahoney

COVER AND INTERIOR DESIGNER
Connor Chin

COPY EDITOR
Melissa Bryan

ILLUSTRATOR
Christine Erikson

Contents

Introduction

As a quilter, one of my favorite things is fabric. I think most of us would agree that fabric sparked our first attraction to quilting. We saw all the fantastic designs and colors, and we oohed and aahed over their beauty. Eventually, we gave in and started buying bits of fabric. Gradually the bits got bigger and bigger, and soon we had a stash! (We all have stashes, don't we?)

My stash is quite large, and a big part of it consists of black-and-white prints. I started collecting them around 1993 when I first began quilting. Since then, my treasure trove of black-and-white prints has blossomed and transformed. I have *tons*, to say the least. But you know what I like even more than black-and-white prints? Partnering them with brightly saturated colors! So I have lots of those fabrics in my stash, too.

When I combine black and white with bright fabrics, something magical happens. My heart begins to sing. It's like eating candy—I want more. I hope the projects in this book will affect you the same way. In these pages you'll find quilts that combine black-and-white prints with vividly colored fabrics to create simply beautiful designs.

I will walk you through selecting fabrics, as well as using specialty tools and techniques. The projects will include paper foundation piecing, curved piecing, strip piecing, and even a little bit of appliqué. Find out what scale of black-and-white prints to use and how to choose the best and brightest fabrics to complement them. So come and take this journey with me, and let's make our hearts sing!

Working with Black-and-White Prints

Designing a quilt using black-and-white prints brings a new level of enjoyment to choosing a color palette. What I like most is that black-and-white prints make all other colors shine. Whether you are choosing pinks, greens, blues, yellows, or browns, they all become the stars of the show.

Prints with black backgrounds make any saturated colors absolutely "pop." White background prints can do the same, with the added potential of giving a quilt a more modern look. It's important to clarify here—when I talk about prints that are black and white, I mean whites that are white *only*. Stay away from prints with cream backgrounds, which can give the quilt a yellow cast when placed next to a white print or solid. And avoid gray prints and solids as well. Gray will dull the intensity of the other colors in the quilt.

One of the things you'll see throughout this book is that I use a variety of black-and-white prints in every quilt. This not only gives each quilt a scrappier look, but also makes the final result more interesting. How much variety to use is up to you. Paring back the number of black-and-white prints can give your quilt a more contemporary appeal, which is apparent in the alternate versions of "Proud Mary" on page 11 and "Twirling" on page 75.

The scale of the black-and-white print is also very important to the design. In many of the quilts, I used small- to medium-scale motifs. The prints I chose were based on the size of the quilt block and the size of the pieces within the block. If the scale of the print is too large, then you might not even see the design of the fabric. Reserve large-scale prints for quilt projects that can feature them in a bigger area. "Crossroads" on page 33 is a perfect example. Since the design includes large squares, I incorporated a mix of both large- and small-scale prints; alternatively, you could use only large-scale motifs for a totally different look. Choosing large-scale prints for "Seeing Spots" on page 23, "No Snowballs Here" on page 59, and the main version of "Twirling" on page 71 could change the look of those quilts as well.

An array of black-and-white prints

6

In "No Snowballs Here," the block centers feature a variety of medium- to large-scale prints. Compare that quilt to the alternate version on page 63, which uses small- to medium-scale prints instead. The different scales of prints give each of the quilts a different feel, and reversing the background prints from white to black gives the quilt a completely new look.

Before you begin a design, I recommend making a test block to audition the fabrics and make sure you like the scale of the prints. Also, try both white and black prints; you may like one version better than the other. The scale of your fabrics really does play a big role in achieving the look you seek.

When you start pairing colors with black-and-white prints, you'll notice differences in what appeals to you. Highly saturated colors, such as hot pink, will stand out vividly against the black-and-white prints. If you want a slightly subdued effect (some quilters call this low-volume), choose less saturated colors, such as pale pink.

Changing the values in the quilt can also have a dramatic impact on the overall appearance. The primarily white background in "Star Bright" on page 39 gives the quilt a very different look and feel than the black background in the alternate version on page 45. In the original quilt, printed fabrics were used in the stars, adding movement to the design. The alternate version uses solid fabrics for the stars, which gives it a more modern look.

Print scale is just as crucial when choosing colored prints as it is for selecting black-and-white prints. When deciding on colored fabrics, consider the overall look and feel you are going for. Solid fabrics read differently than prints. Using solids in the alternate version of "Climbing Mountains" on page 32, instead of the mottled and printed batiks in the main version on page 27, changes the look of the quilt substantially.

In "Lava Lamps" on page 13 and "Dreaming of Pyramids" on page 65, I used multicolored prints with either black or white backgrounds. I was very selective when choosing the prints; they were mostly small in scale with some type of dot, and they all incorporated the full rainbow spectrum of colors, not just one color. Choosing multicolored prints adds a huge amount of interest to a quilt. Fair warning, though—I collected these fabrics over many years.

Multicolored prints with black or white backgrounds

One of the best things about quilting is that we get to play with fabric. Here is your chance to experiment and see what appeals to you the most. You are *not* locked in to a certain collection of fabrics. You have the freedom to choose from many fabrics to achieve the look and feel you want. Scrappy, modern, bold, subdued, a traditional twist—you name it, the sky is the limit! So reach for the sky and give your inner designer a chance to play.

"Proud Mary," pieced by Jackie Kunkel
and quilted by Margaret Solomon Gunn

Finished quilt: 60½" x 60½"
Finished blocks: 6" x 6"

Proud Mary

You know the song, now meet the quilt—a tribute to my grandmother, who has been gone for years but is missed every single day. She WAS Proud Mary!

Materials

Yardage is based on 42"-wide fabric.

⅜ yard *each* of 12 assorted black prints for blocks

⅜ yard *each* of 12 assorted white prints for blocks

⅛ yard *each* of 4 assorted purple, yellow, green, blue, turquoise, red, and orange prints for blocks

½ yard of black solid for binding

4¼ yards of fabric for backing

68" x 68" piece of batting

Template plastic

Cutting

From the assorted black prints, cut:
8 strips, 4½" x 42"; crosscut into 50 rectangles, 4½" x 5½"

12 strips, 6¾" x 42"

From the assorted white prints, cut:
8 strips, 4½" x 42"; crosscut into 50 rectangles, 4½" x 5½"

12 strips, 6¾" x 42"

From *each* of the assorted purple, yellow, green, blue, turquoise, red, and orange prints, cut:
1 strip, 1½" x 42"; crosscut into 4 rectangles, 1½" x 5½" (112 total; 12 will be left over)

From the black solid, cut:
7 strips, 2¼" x 42"

Making the Blocks

While it looks like this quilt is made using circle blocks, plus partial circles around the perimeter, it's actually constructed of quarter-circle blocks, allowing you more freedom to arrange the elements of your quilt top as desired.

1 Pair each colored rectangle, right sides together, with a black or white rectangle and sew together along their long edges to make 100 units. Press the seam allowances toward the colored print.

Make 100.

2 Trace the A and B patterns on page 12 onto template plastic. Cut out both templates on the marked lines.

3 Position template A on a unit from step 1, with one straight edge of the template along the bottom edge of the colored rectangle as shown. Trace around the template. Trace 50 white and 50 black A units.

4 Cut out the A units using a rotary cutter and ruler to cut the straight edges. Cut the curved edges either freehand with a rotary cutter that has a *new* blade, or with very sharp scissors.

Cutting Curves

If you choose to cut the curves with a rotary cutter, use a 60 mm cutter, as it has more surface area and lets you make a smoother cut.

5 Trace the B template 50 times onto the black 6¾"-wide strips. Trace another 50 B shapes onto the white 6¾"-wide strips. Cut out the units as described in step 4.

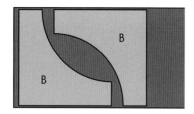

6 Refer to the photo on page 8 and the quilt layout below right for placement guidance as needed. Arrange the A and B units on a design wall, pairing white A units with black B units and vice versa. Rearrange the units until you are pleased with the appearance.

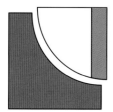 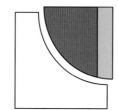

Pair opposite-color A and B units.

7 Referring to "Curved Piecing Technique" on page 77, sew the A and B units together. Press the seam allowances toward the B units. Square up the blocks to measure 6½" x 6½". Make 50 of each unit (100 total).

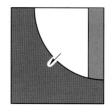 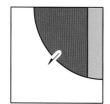

Make 50 of each.

Assembling the Quilt Top

1 Lay out the blocks in 10 rows of 10 blocks each as shown in the quilt layout. The keys to the layout are block placement and rotation. Rotate the quarter-circle blocks to make full circles with a matching-color plus sign in the center of each block.

Assembling the Rows

When assembling this quilt top, color placement is very specific. Each row of blocks makes a half-circle block, so the correct rotation of the blocks is critical to achieving the overall design. To help keep things straight, start in the top-left corner and sew the first two blocks together. Then place them back in the layout and move to the next two blocks. Make sure the overall layout is correct before sewing the rows together. If a block isn't rotated correctly, it's much easier to correct the mistake before joining the rows.

2 Sew the blocks together in rows. Press the seam allowances in opposite directions from row to row. Sew the rows together and press the seam allowances in one direction.

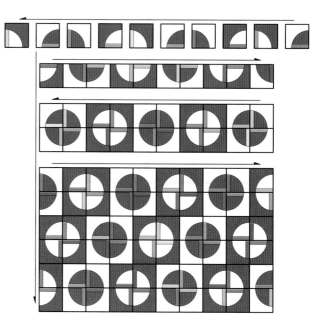

Quilt layout

Finishing the Quilt

For more details on any of the following steps, go to ShopMartingale.com/HowtoQuilt for free downloadable information. If you plan to have your quilt professionally machine quilted, check with the long-arm quilter to see how you should prepare your backing.

1 Press the quilt top. Piece the backing fabric so that it's at least 4" larger than the quilt top on all sides.

2 Layer the quilt top with batting and backing; baste. Quilt as desired. The quilt shown features straight lines in the quarter circles and swirls in the background. Straight lines show up better than swirls do on busier prints. Choose wisely if you want to see the quilting design on a busy print; simple geometric or linear designs will be the most visible.

3 Use the black-solid 2¼"-wide strips to bind your quilt.

Alternate Version

"Proud Mary," pieced by Sally Murray and quilted by Margaret Solomon Gunn. Sally used black and white solids instead of prints to give this version a modern feel. The solids also make a great canvas for some terrific machine quilting!

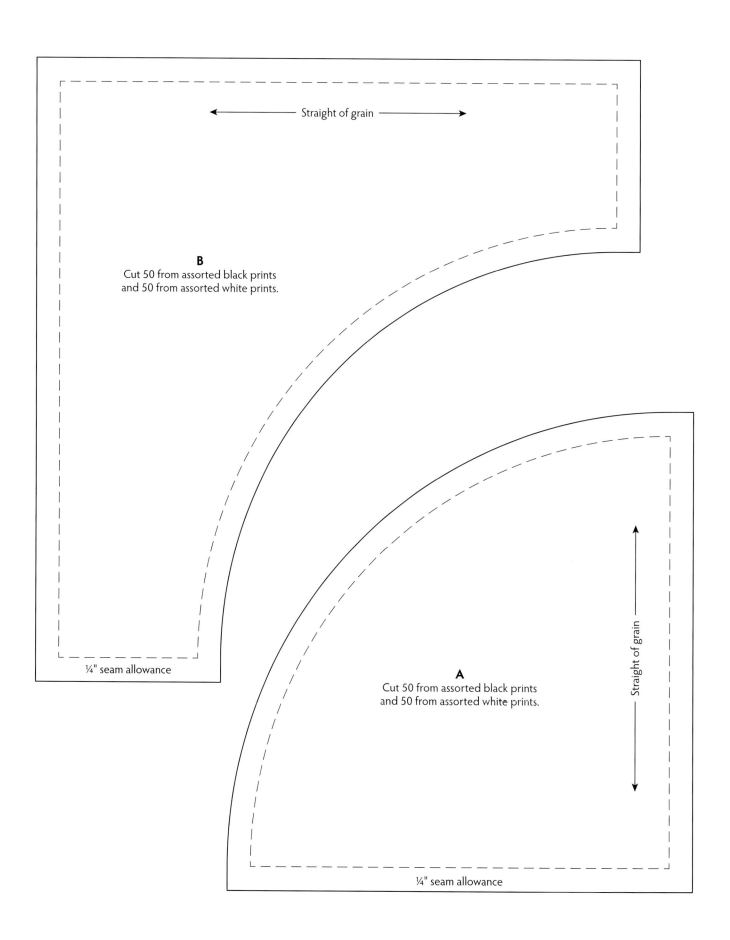

Straight of grain

B
Cut 50 from assorted black prints
and 50 from assorted white prints.

¼" seam allowance

A
Cut 50 from assorted black prints
and 50 from assorted white prints.

Straight of grain

¼" seam allowance

Lava Lamps

Do you remember those psychedelic lights from the 1960s and '70s? They were mesmerizing! I had a few, and what I loved best was the colors and the bulbous shapes the "lava" made when traversing the light.

Materials

Yardage is based on 42"-wide fabric. Fat quarters measure 18" x 21".

14 fat quarters of assorted multicolored prints with white backgrounds for blocks*

14 fat quarters of assorted multicolored prints with black backgrounds for blocks*

½ yard of black print for binding

4¼ yards of fabric for backing

62" x 72" piece of batting

Template plastic

*For a scrappier quilt, use more fat quarters.

Cutting

From the black print for binding, cut:
6 strips, 2¼" x 42"

Making the Units

A design wall is helpful when creating the blocks. Before joining the A and B pieces, I recommend arranging them on a design wall, referring to the photo on page 14 and the quilt layout on page 15 for placement guidance. For ease of reading, prints will be referred to as "black" or "white" in instructions.

1 Trace the A and B patterns on page 17 onto template plastic. Cut out both templates on the marked lines.

2 Position the templates on the black prints and trace 84 A pieces and 36 B pieces.

3 Position the templates on the white prints and trace 36 A pieces and 84 B pieces.

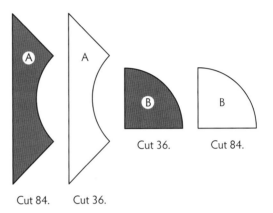

Cut 84. Cut 36. Cut 36. Cut 84.

Fitting the Templates

When tracing the templates onto the prints, try to fit as many A and B pieces as you can onto each fat quarter. This will maximize your fabric and give you more variety to choose from when you lay out the blocks. Variety makes for a much more interesting quilt.

4 Cut out the A and B pieces using a rotary cutter and ruler to cut the straight edges. Cut the curved edges freehand with a rotary cutter that has a *new* blade, or with very sharp scissors.

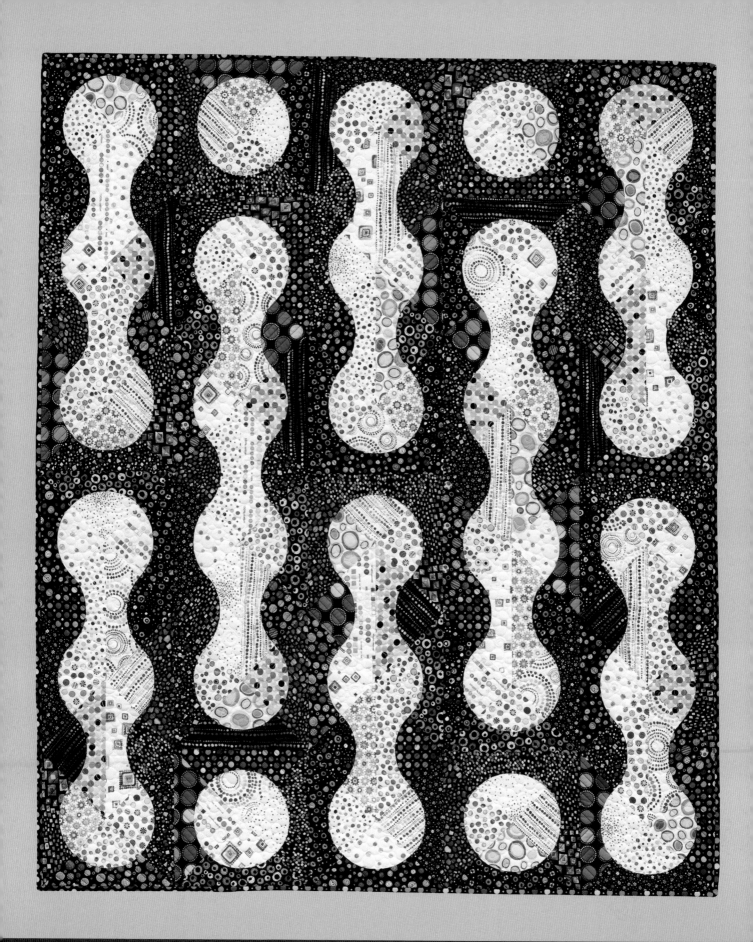

"Lava Lamps," pieced by Jackie Kunkel
and quilted by Margaret Solomon Gun

Finished quilt: 53½" x 64¼"

5 Referring to the quilt layout, arrange the A and B pieces on a design wall, pairing the white A pieces with the black B pieces and vice versa. Rearrange the pieces until you are pleased with the appearance.

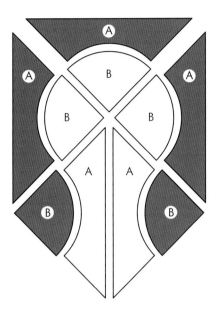

Use a Design Wall

I like to arrange the individual A and B pieces on my design wall to preview the placement of the fabrics. This allows me to reposition pieces before I sew them together, and I can make sure I don't end up with like fabrics next to each other.

6 Referring to "Curved Piecing Technique" on page 77, sew the A and B pieces together. Press the seam allowances toward the A pieces. Make 84 units using black A pieces and 36 units using white A pieces.

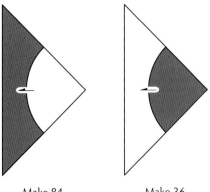

Make 84.   Make 36.

Assembling the Quilt Top

1 Arrange the units in diagonal rows as shown in the quilt layout below. Sew the units together in rows. Press the seam allowances in opposite directions from row to row.

2 Sew the rows together and press the seam allowances in one direction.

Quilt layout

Creating a New Design

Come up with your own new and exciting creation by simply moving the units around on the design wall. The construction of the rows will remain the same, but now *you're* the designer!

Finishing the Quilt

For more details on any of the following steps, go to ShopMartingale.com/HowtoQuilt for free downloadable information. If you plan to have your quilt professionally machine quilted, check with the long-arm quilter to see how you should prepare your backing.

1. Press the quilt top. Piece the backing fabric so that it's at least 4" larger than the quilt top on all sides.

2. Layer the quilt top with batting and backing; baste. Quilt as desired. The quilt shown was quilted with a combination of pebbles and straight lines.

3. Use the black-print 2¼"-wide strips to bind your quilt.

Choosing Quilting Designs

When you use a printed fabric, you're much less likely to see the actual quilting stitches on the quilt. If you'd like the quilting to show, it's best to use a simple design, such as straight lines. Most of the time, a simple allover design is sufficient for busy prints.

Alternate Version

"Lava Lamps," pieced and quilted by Caroline Berman. Caroline was simply asked to create her own black-and-white interpretation of the original design. She creatively decided to make columns of black and white, with red prints added to the mix to represent the "lava."

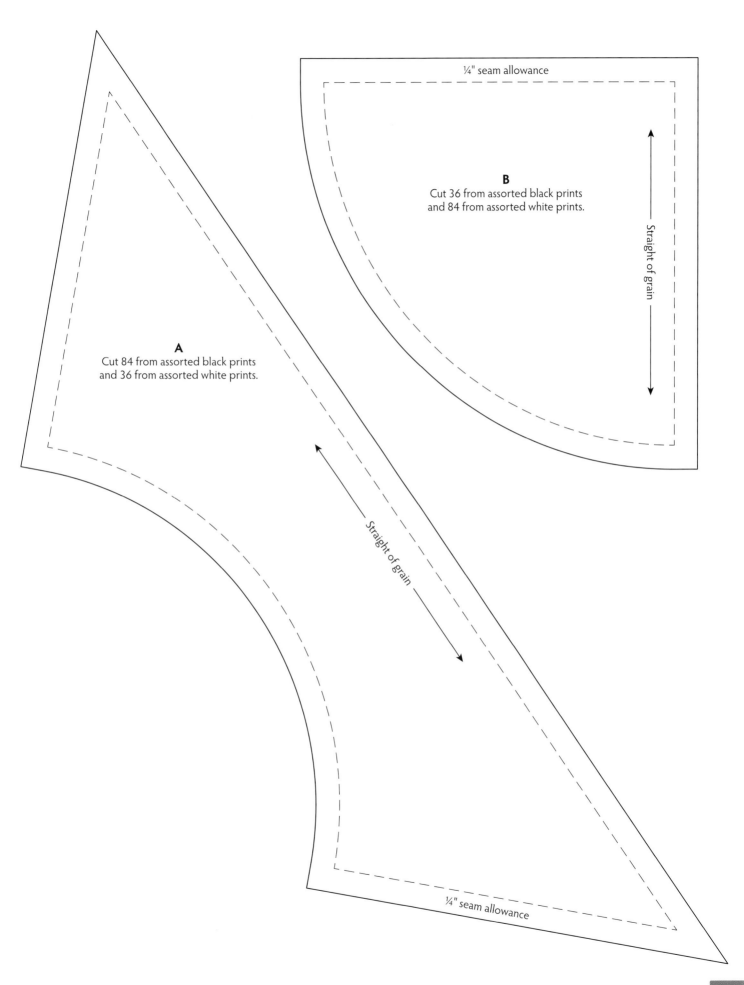

¼" seam allowance

B
Cut 36 from assorted black prints
and 84 from assorted white prints.

Straight of grain

A
Cut 84 from assorted black prints
and 36 from assorted white prints.

Straight of grain

¼" seam allowance

"It's a Celebration," pieced
and quilted by Jackie Kunkel

Finished table runner: 20½" x 50½"
Finished place mat: 12½" x 18½"
Finished block: 4" x 10"

It's a Celebration
Table Runner and Place Mats

Everyone loves a celebration, right? Break out the party ware and set the table for some fun! Birthdays, Cinco de Mayo, graduations—whatever the occasion, make it extra fun with a brightly set table.

Materials

Yardage is based on 42"-wide fabric and is sufficient to make 1 table runner and 6 place mats.

⅓ yard *each* of 11 assorted black prints for blocks and borders

¼ yard *each* of 11 assorted white prints for blocks and borders

19 strips, 2½" x 21", of assorted bright prints for blocks and table-runner corner squares

1⅛ yards of multicolored stripe for binding

3¾ yards of fabric for backing

6 pieces, 18" x 24", of batting for place mats

1 piece, 28" x 58", of batting for table runner

Template plastic

Cutting

From *each* of the assorted white prints, cut:
  1 strip, 2½" x 42"; crosscut into 2 strips, 2½" x 21" (22 total; 3 will be left over)

  1 strip, 4½" x 42" (11 total)

From *each* of the assorted black prints, cut:
  1 strip, 4½" x 42" (11 total)

From the remainder of the assorted black prints, cut a *total* of:
  12 strips, 1½" x 42"; crosscut *9 of the strips* into:

  14 strips, 1½" x 10½"

  12 strips, 1½" x 14½"

From the multicolored stripe, cut:
  15 strips, 2¼" x 42"

Making the Blocks

1. Pair a white 2½"-wide strip with a bright strip. With right sides together, sew the strips together along their long edges. Press the seam allowances toward the bright strip. Repeat to make a total of 19 strip sets. Cut the strip sets into 2½"-wide segments, for a total of 148; you'll need 58 segments for the table runner and 90 segments for the place mats (15 for each mat).

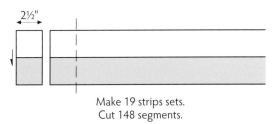

Make 19 strips sets.
Cut 148 segments.

2. Select five different segments from step 1. Lay them out as shown, making sure the bright squares create a checkerboard pattern. Sew the segments together to make a checkerboard unit. Press the seam allowances in one direction. Make 10 units for the table runner and 18 units for the place mats (3 for each mat). You'll have eight segments left over to make Four Patch corner squares for the table runner.

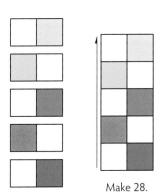

Make 28.

3 Sew 10 units together as shown to make the table runner. Press the seam allowances in one direction. The table runner should measure 10½" x 40½".

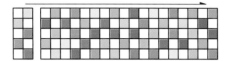

4 For each place mat, sew three units together as shown. Press the seam allowances in one direction. Each place mat should measure 10½" x 12½". Make a total of six.

Make 6.

Adding the Inner Borders

1 For the table runner, sew black 1½" x 10½" strips to each short end. Press the seam allowances toward the black strips. Join the three black 1½" x 42" strips end to end to make a strip at least 86" long. From the pieced strip, cut two 42½"-long strips and sew them to the long edges of the table runner. Press the seam allowances toward the black strips. The table runner should measure 12½" x 42½".

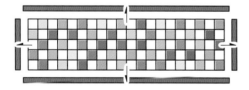

2 For each place mat, sew black 1½" x 10½" strips to each short end. Press the seam allowances toward the black strips. Then sew black 1½" x 14½" strips to the long edges of each place mat. Press the seam allowances toward the black strips. Each place mat should measure 12½" x 14½". Make a total of six.

Adding the Pieced Borders

1 Trace the triangle pattern on page 21 onto template plastic and cut out on the marked lines.

2 Using the triangle template and the 4½"-wide strips of black and white prints, trace 116 black and 116 white pieces. Use a rotary cutter and ruler to cut out the pieces.

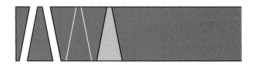

3 Place the table runner on a design wall and arrange 26 black and 26 white triangles along each long side, alternating the pieces as shown. Then place eight black and eight white triangles on each short side. Rearrange the triangles until you are pleased with the appearance. Sew the triangles in each row together to make a border strip. Press the seam allowances in one direction. Trim the 16-piece border strips to measure 12½" long. Trim the 52-piece border strips to measure 42½" long.

Trim ends.

Make 2.

Make 2.

Joining the Pieces

To join the triangles, place black and white pieces right sides together, offsetting them so you can see little "dog ears" overhanging each piece. Offsetting the triangles will allow you to sew straight border strips.

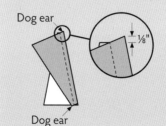

Dog ear

Dog ear

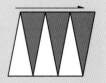

4 Lay out two of the remaining segments from step 1 of "Making the Blocks" as shown. Join the segments to make a Four Patch block. Press the seam allowances in one direction. Make a total of four blocks.

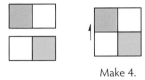

Make 4.

5 Sew the 12½"-long border strips to the short sides of the table runner. Press the seam allowances toward the inner border. Sew Four Patch blocks to the ends of each 42½"-long border strip and press the seam allowances toward the Four Patch blocks. Sew these borders to the long sides of the table runner. Press the seam allowances toward the inner border.

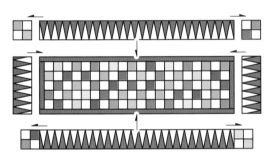

Table-runner layout

6 For each place mat, position eight black and eight white triangles on one short side of the mat, alternating the black and white pieces as shown in the place-mat layout below. Sew the triangles together to make a border strip. Press the seam allowances in one direction. Trim the border strip to measure 12½" long. Make six border strips.

7 Sew a border strip from step 6 to one short side of each place mat. Press the seam allowances toward the inner border.

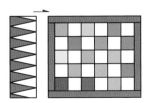

Place-mat layout

Finishing the Table Runner and Place Mats

For more details on any of the following steps, go to ShopMartingale.com/HowtoQuilt for free downloadable information. If you plan to have your table runner and place mats professionally machine quilted, check with the long-arm quilter to see how you should prepare your backing.

1 Press the table runner and place mats. Cut the backing fabric so it's at least 4" larger than the table runner and each place mat on all sides.

2 Layer the table runner and each place mat with batting and backing; baste. Quilt as desired. The table runner and place mats shown were quilted with an allover design of random circles.

3 Use the multicolored-stripe 2¼"-wide strips to bind your table runner and place mats.

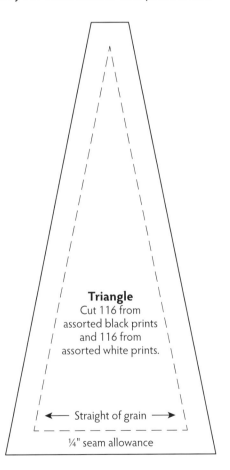

Triangle
Cut 116 from assorted black prints and 116 from assorted white prints.

← Straight of grain →

¼" seam allowance

"Seeing Spots," pieced by Jackie Kunkel and quilted by Pamela Burnham

Finished quilt: 78½" x 91½"

Seeing Spots

Some call them spots, others call them dots, but whatever you call them, they are FUN! They add whimsy to anything, which probably explains why we see them popping up everywhere.

Materials
Yardage is based on 42"-wide fabric.

¾ yard *each* of 6 assorted polka-dot prints for triangles

¾ yard *each* of 6 assorted black prints for triangles

¾ yard *each* of 6 assorted white prints for triangles

¾ yard of black solid for binding

7¼ yards of fabric for backing

86" x 99" piece of batting

Template plastic or 60° triangle ruler

Cutting

From *each* of the polka-dot, white, and black prints, cut:
3 strips, 6⅝" x 42" (54 total)

From the black solid for binding, cut:
9 strips, 2¼" x 42"

Use a Ruler

Although template patterns have been provided for your convenience, I prefer using a Creative Grids 60° ruler for this project. There are many rulers available, so test them out to find the one you like best, and give it a whirl with this fun quilt.

Assembling the Quilt Top

This quilt appears to be made by creating hexagons from the 60° triangles and then sewing everything together. However, the triangles are actually joined in vertical columns so no set-in seams are required!

1 Trace the A and B patterns on page 26 onto template plastic. Cut out both templates on the marked lines.

2 Position the A template on a black strip, aligning the top and bottom edges of the template with the edges of the strips. Trace a total of 112 A triangles onto the black strips. Use a rotary cutter and ruler to cut out the triangles. Repeat to trace and cut 113 white A triangles and 100 polka-dot A triangles.

3 Using the B template and the remaining black strips, trace four triangles on the *right* side of the strips and four triangles on the *wrong* side of the strips. Cut out all triangles.

Make 4 of each.

4 Repeating step 3, trace and cut five white B triangles and five white B reversed triangles. In the same way, cut four polka-dot B triangles and four polka-dot B reversed triangles.

5 On a design wall, lay out the A and B triangles in 13 columns as shown in the quilt layout below. Rearrange the white and black A triangles until you are pleased with the appearance.

6 Sew the triangles together in columns. Press the seam allowances open. Sew the columns together and press the seam allowances open.

Quilt layout

Pressing Pointer

In this quilt, pressing the seam allowances open helps achieve accurate points and helps the quilt lie flatter than if the seam allowances were pressed to one side.

Finishing the Quilt

For more details on any of the following steps, go to ShopMartingale.com/HowtoQuilt for free downloadable information. If you plan to have your quilt professionally machine quilted, check with the long-arm quilter to see how you should prepare your backing.

1 Press the quilt top. Piece the backing fabric so that it's at least 6" larger than the quilt top.

2 Layer the quilt top with batting and backing; baste. Quilt as desired. This quilt was quilted with a distinctive design of swirls, curves, and circles.

3 Use the black solid 2¼"-wide strips to bind your quilt.

Alternate Version

"Seeing Spots," pieced by Fran Adams and quilted by Jackie Kunkel. Fran was excused from "seeing spots" for her interpretation of this design; instead, she was asked to create a black-and-white version with a rainbow of brights, but to mix it up. The result is a totally different design. Even though 60° triangles are still part of the construction, no hexagons were formed because of the way the fabrics were positioned. (Fran cut 100 each of white, black, and colored triangles.)

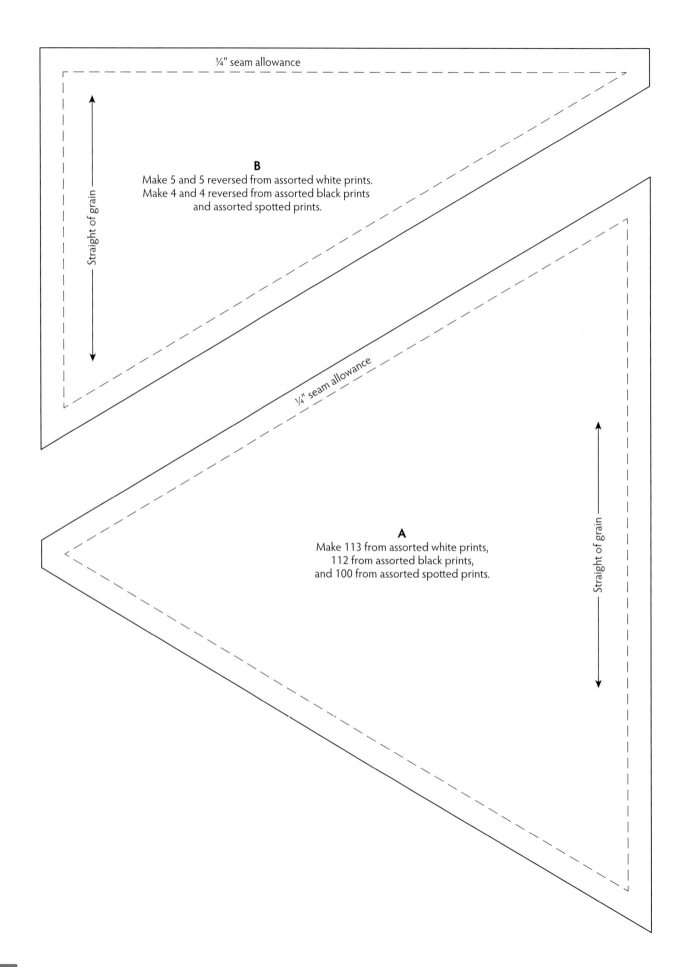

¼" seam allowance

Straight of grain

B
Make 5 and 5 reversed from assorted white prints.
Make 4 and 4 reversed from assorted black prints
and assorted spotted prints.

¼" seam allowance

Straight of grain

A
Make 113 from assorted white prints,
112 from assorted black prints,
and 100 from assorted spotted prints.

Climbing Mountains

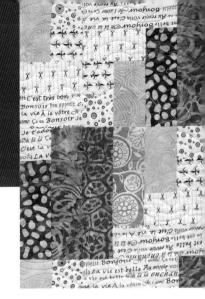

My husband and I love to hike and climb. The stair-step nature of the blocks in this quilt remind me of when we climbed the mountains in Peru. But more so, this quilt is made with my husband in mind . . . he climbed and reached the summit of Mt. Kilimanjaro in 2005! So, let's go climb some mountains.

Materials

Yardage is based on 42"-wide fabric.

⅜ yard *each* of white prints #1 and #2 for Log Cabin blocks

½ yard of white print #3 for Log Cabin blocks and corner blocks

⅝ yard of white print #4 for Log Cabin blocks and corner blocks

½ yard *each* of white prints #5 and #6 for border blocks

⅛ yard of white print #7 for corner blocks

⅛ yard *each* of black prints #1 and #2 for corner blocks

½ yard *each* of purple print and black print #3 for border blocks

½ yard *each* of red, yellow, and blue prints for Log Cabin blocks

⅜ yard *each* of orange and green prints for Log Cabin blocks

½ yard of black print #4 for binding

4¼ yards of fabric for backing

72" x 72" piece of batting

Make It Scrappier

This quilt was made entirely of 2½"-wide strips. Instead of going for a planned look, use precut strips from your stash and mix things up to make it scrappy! The alternate version on page 32 was made from scraps and a Kona Cotton Solids roll-up. Make it your own!

Cutting

From *each* of white prints #1 and #2, cut:
3 strips, 2½" x 42"; crosscut into 36 squares, 2½" x 2½" (72 total)

From the yellow print, cut:
5 strips, 2½" x 42"; crosscut into 36 rectangles, 2½" x 4½"

From white print #3, cut:
6 strips, 2½" x 42"; crosscut into:
40 rectangles, 2½" x 4½"
4 rectangles, 2½" x 6½"

From *each* of the green and orange prints, cut:
3 strips, 2½" x 42"; crosscut into 18 rectangles, 2½" x 6½" (36 total)

From white print #4, cut:
7 strips, 2½" x 42"; crosscut into:
36 rectangles, 2½" x 6½"
4 squares, 2½" x 2½"

From *each* of the blue and red prints, cut:
5 strips, 2½" x 42"; crosscut into 18 rectangles, 2½" x 8½" (36 total)

From black print #1, cut:
1 strip, 2½" x 42"; crosscut into:
4 rectangles, 2½" x 6½"
4 squares, 2½" x 2½"

From black print #2, cut:
4 rectangles, 2½" x 4½"

From white print #7, cut:
1 strip, 2½" x 42"; crosscut into 4 rectangles, 2½" x 8½"

(Continued on page 29)

"Climbing Mountains," pieced by Jackie Kunkel
and quilted by Pamela Burnham

Finished quilt: 64½" x 64½"
Finished blocks: 8" x 8" and 8" x 16"

(Continued from page 27)

From *each* of white prints #5 and #6, cut:
   6 strips, 2½" x 42"; crosscut into 12 rectangles, 2½" x 16½" (24 total)

From black print #3, cut:
   6 strips, 2½" x 42"; crosscut into 12 rectangles, 2½" x 16½"

From the purple print, cut:
   6 strips, 2½" x 42"; crosscut into 12 rectangles, 2½" x 16½"

From black print #4, cut:
   7 strips, 2¼" x 42"

Making the Quarter Log Cabin Blocks

1 Sew a white #1 square to a white #2 square to make a two-patch unit. Press the seam allowances in one direction. Make 36 identical units.

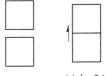

Make 36.

2 Sew a yellow rectangle to each unit from step 1 as shown. Press the seam allowances toward the yellow rectangle. Make 36 units.

Make 36.

3 Sew a 2½" x 4½" white #3 rectangle to the top of each unit from step 2. Press the seam allowances toward the white rectangle. Make 36 units.

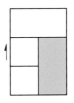

Make 36.

4 Sew a green rectangle to each unit from step 3 as shown. Press the seam allowances toward the green rectangle. Make 18 units. Set aside the remaining 18 units from step 3 to use in step 7.

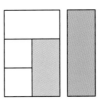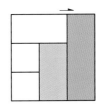

Make 18.

5 Sew a white #4 rectangle to each unit from step 4 as shown. Press the seam allowances toward the white rectangle. Make 18 units.

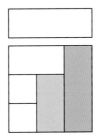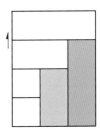

Make 18.

6 Sew a blue rectangle to each unit from step 5 as shown to make block A. Press the seam allowances toward the blue rectangle. Make 18 blocks.

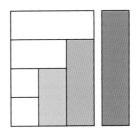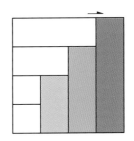

Block A.
Make 18.

Chain Piecing

Chain piecing the units speeds up the process greatly. In each step, just add the same rectangle to the same unit over and over until you've made all of the units. Then move on to the next step, and before you know it, all your blocks will be complete!

7 Using the remaining units from step 3, repeat steps 4–6 with the orange rectangles in place of the green rectangles and the red rectangles in place of the blue rectangles. Make 18 B blocks.

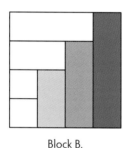

Block B.
Make 18.

Making the Corner Blocks

Press the seam allowances toward the just-added rectangle throughout.

1 Sew a white #4 square to a black #1 square to make a two-patch unit. Press the seam allowances in one direction. Make four identical units. Sew a 2½" x 4½" white #3 rectangle to each unit as shown.

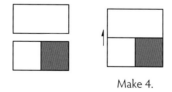

Make 4.

2 Sew a black #2 rectangle to each unit from step 1 as shown. Then add a black #1 rectangle. Make four units.

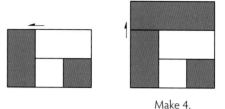

Make 4.

3 Sew a 2½" x 6½" white #3 rectangle to each unit from step 2 as shown. Then add a white #7 rectangle to complete the block. Make four blocks.

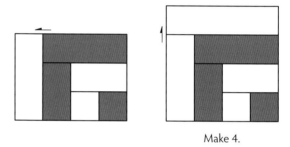

Make 4.

Making the Border Blocks

Join a white #5 rectangle, a white #6 rectangle, a black #3 rectangle, and a purple rectangle along their long edges as shown to make a block. Press the seam allowances in one direction. The block should measure 8½" x 16½". Make 12 blocks.

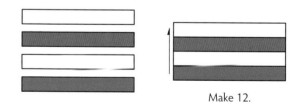

Make 12.

Pieced Border

Constructing the borders from blocks, instead of long strips, gives you more design flexibility. You can make the border blocks scrappy or uniform, as I did. All of the blocks are joined in rows, so there is no need to add traditional borders—a very cool way to create the look of a border without having to make one, and much easier too!

Assembling the Quilt Top

1 On a design wall, lay out the A and B Quarter Log Cabin blocks in six rows of six blocks each, rotating the B blocks as shown in the quilt layout at right. Place the border blocks around the outside edges. Add the corner blocks, rotating them as needed.

2 Sew the Quarter Log Cabin blocks together into rows. Press the seam allowances in opposite directions from row to row. Then sew the rows together in pairs to make three 16½" x 48½" rows. Press the seam allowances in one direction. Return the pairs of rows to your design wall.

3 Sew border blocks to the ends of each row from step 2. Press the seam allowances in the directions indicated.

4 Join the border blocks and corner blocks in the top row to make the top border. Press the seam allowances in the directions indicated. Join the border blocks and corner blocks in the bottom row to make the bottom border. Press.

5 Sew the rows and borders from steps 3 and 4 together to complete the quilt top. Press the seam allowances in the directions indicated.

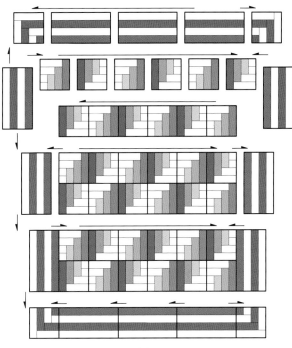

Quilt layout

Finishing the Quilt

For more details on any of the following steps, go to ShopMartingale.com/HowtoQuilt for free downloadable information. If you plan to have your quilt professionally machine quilted, check with the long-arm quilter to see how you should prepare your backing.

1 Press the quilt top. Piece the backing fabric so that it's at least 4" larger than the quilt top on all sides.

2 Layer the quilt top with batting and backing; baste. Quilt as desired. This quilt was quilted with an allover swirl design.

3 Use the black #4 strips to bind your quilt.

"Climbing Mountains," pieced by Roberta Stoddard and quilted by Pamela Burnham. In this version, Roberta used black prints as the background instead of white prints, and incorporated bright solids instead of prints or batiks. Using different fabrics gives this quilt a distinctive look.

Crossroads

Have you ever been at a crossroads in your life? I have, both literally and figuratively! When I'm at a crossroads, I always look toward the path that seems most positive, and that's where I begin my journey. Where will your "Crossroads" take you?

Materials

Yardage is based on 42"-wide fabric.

⅓ yard *each* of red, purple, bright-yellow, and blue prints for center block and flying-geese strips

⅛ yard of white print #1 for center block

1 yard of white print #2 for pieced border and setting squares and triangles

½ yard *each* of white prints #3 and #4 for setting squares and triangles

⅓ yard *each* of white prints #5 and #6 for setting squares

¼ yard of black print #1 for center block and flying-geese strips

Scrap of black print #2 for center block

¾ yard of black print #3 for flying-geese strips and pieced border

½ yard of black print #4 for binding

½ yard of pale-yellow print for flying-geese strips

⅓ yard of orange print for flying-geese strips and corner triangles

⅓ yard of green print for center block, flying-geese strips, and corner triangles

3½ yards of fabric for backing

59" x 59" piece of batting

Template plastic

Cutting

From white print #1, cut:

1 strip, 2¼" x 42"; crosscut into 12 squares, 2¼" x 2¼". Cut each square in half diagonally to yield 24 triangles.

From black print #1, cut:

3 strips, 1⅞" x 42"; crosscut into:

12 rectangles, 1⅞" x 8½"

4 squares, 1⅞" x 1⅞"

From the green print, cut:

1 square, 6½" x 6½"; cut into quarters diagonally to yield 4 triangles

1 square, 6½" x 6½"; cut in half diagonally to yield 2 triangles

2 squares, 3½" x 3½"; cut in half diagonally to yield 4 triangles

From the orange print, cut:

2 squares, 6½" x 6½"; cut into quarters diagonally to yield 8 triangles

1 square, 6½" x 6½"; cut in half diagonally to yield 2 triangles

1 square, 3⅞" x 3⅞"; cut into quarters diagonally to yield 4 triangles

From the red print, cut:

2 squares, 6½" x 6½"; cut into quarters diagonally to yield 8 triangles

1 square, 3⅞" x 3⅞"; cut into quarters diagonally to yield 4 triangles

1 square, 3½" x 3½"

(Continued on page 35)

"Crossroads," pieced by Jackie Kunkel and quilted by Margaret Solomon Gunn

Finished quilt: 51¾" x 51¾"
Finished block: 8" x 8"

(Continued from page 33)

From black print #2, cut:
1 square, 3⅛" x 3⅛"

From the bright-yellow print, cut:
2 squares, 6½" x 6½"; cut into quarters diagonally to yield 8 triangles

1 square, 3½" x 3½"

From the pale-yellow print, cut:
4 strips, 3½" x 42"; crosscut into 36 squares, 3½" x 3½". Cut each square in half diagonally to yield 72 triangles.

From *each* of the purple and blue prints, cut:
1 square, 6½" x 6½"; cut into quarters diagonally to yield 4 triangles (8 total)

1 square, 3½" x 3½" (2 total)

From black print #3, cut:
4 strips, 3½" x 42"

3 strips, 1⅞" x 42"; crosscut into 12 rectangles, 1⅞" x 8½"

From white print #2, cut:
1 strip, 3⅝" x 42"; crosscut into 4 rectangles, 3⅝" x 9⅛"

4 strips, 3½" x 42"

2 squares, 12½" x 12½"; cut into quarters diagonally to yield 4 triangles

1 square, 8½" x 8½"

From white print #5, cut:
3 squares, 8½" x 8½"

From white print #6, cut:
4 squares, 8½" x 8½"

From white print #3, cut:
1 square, 12½" x 12½"; cut into quarters diagonally to yield 4 triangles

2 squares, 8½" x 8½"

From white print #4, cut:
1 square, 12½" x 12½"; cut into quarters diagonally to yield 4 triangles

1 square, 8½" x 8½"

From black print #4 , cut:
6 strips, 2¼" x 42"

Making the Center Block

1 Sew white #1 triangles to adjacent sides of a black #1 square as shown to make a triangle unit. Press the seam allowances toward the black square. Make four units.

Make 4.

2 Sew a green 3½" triangle to each unit from step 1 as shown. Press the seam allowances toward the green triangle. Make four units.

Make 4.

3 Sew white #1 triangles to the short sides of an orange 3⅞" triangle as shown to make a flying-geese unit. Press the seam allowances toward the white triangles. Make four units.

Make 4.

4 Sew white #1 triangles to the short sides of a red 3⅞" triangle as shown to make a flying-geese unit. Press the seam allowances toward the white triangles. Make four units.

Make 4.

5 Sew the orange and red flying-geese units together in pairs. Press the seam allowances toward the orange unit. Make four units.

Make 4.

6 Lay out the black #2 square and the units from steps 2 and 5 in three rows as shown. Sew the pieces together in rows. Press the seam allowances in opposite directions from row to row. Sew the rows together and press the seam allowances in one direction.

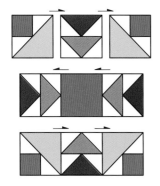

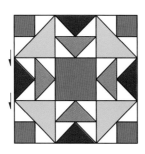

Center block.
Make 1.

Making the Flying-Geese Blocks

1 Sew pale-yellow triangles to the short sides of a red 6½" triangle as shown to make a flying-geese unit. Press the seam allowances toward the pale-yellow triangles. Make eight units.

Make 8.

2 Repeat step 1, sewing pale-yellow triangles to the orange 6½" triangles to make eight flying-geese units. Then sew pale-yellow triangles to the bright-yellow 6½" triangles to make eight units.

Make 8 of each.

3 Repeat step 1, sewing pale-yellow triangles to the green 6½" triangles to make four flying-geese units. Sew pale-yellow triangles to the blue triangles to make four units. Then sew pale-yellow triangles to the purple triangles to make four units.

Make 4 of each.

4 Sew one red, one orange, and one yellow flying-geese unit together as shown to make a strip. Press the seam allowances in the direction indicated. Make eight units.

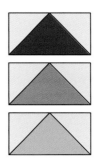
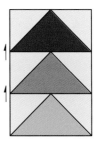

Make 8.

5 Sew one green, one blue, and one purple flying-geese unit together as shown to make a strip. Press the seam allowances in the direction indicated. Make four units.

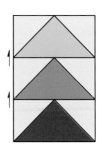

Make 4.

6 Sew a black #1 rectangle to the left side of each strip from step 4. Press the seam allowances toward the black strip. Sew a black #3 rectangle to the right side of each strip to complete the block. Make eight blocks.

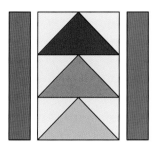 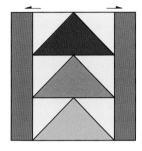

Make 8.

7 Sew a black #1 rectangle to the left side of each strip from step 5. Press the seam allowances toward the black strip. Sew a black #3 rectangle to the right side of each strip to complete the block. Make four blocks.

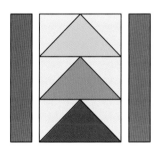 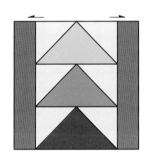

Make 4.

Making the Pieced Border

This unique border is created using a template.

1 Trace the A pattern on page 38 onto template plastic. Cut out the template on the marked lines.

2 Using the A template and the black #3 strips, trace 12 A triangles. Use a rotary cutter and ruler to cut out the triangles. In the same way, trace and cut out eight white #2 A triangles.

3 Place two white #2 rectangles *wrong* sides together and cut them diagonally as shown to make four B triangles. In the same way, cut the remaining pair of white #2 rectangles to make a total of eight B triangles.

Cut 8 B triangles.

4 Lay out three black A triangles, two white A triangles, and two B triangles from step 3 as shown. Join the triangles and press the seam allowances toward the black triangles. Make a total of four border strips.

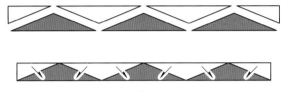

Make 4.

5 Referring to the quilt layout on page 38 for placement guidance, sew a blue square and a red square to the ends of one border strip from step 4. Sew a yellow square and a purple square to the ends of a second border strip from step 4. Press all seam allowances toward the squares.

Assembling the Quilt Top

1 On a design wall, arrange the blocks, white 8½" squares, and white 12½" triangles in diagonal rows as shown in the quilt layout.

2 Sew the pieces together in diagonal rows. Press the seam allowances in opposite directions from row to row. Sew the rows together. Add the green and orange 6½" corner triangles. Press the seam allowances as indicated by the arrows.

3 Sew the pieced borders to the sides first, and then the top and bottom of the quilt top. Press the seam allowances toward the quilt center.

Quilt layout

Finishing the Quilt

For more details on any of the following steps, go to ShopMartingale.com/HowtoQuilt for free downloadable information. If you plan to have your quilt professionally machine quilted, check with the long-arm quilter to see how you should prepare your backing.

1 Press the quilt top. Piece the backing fabric so that it's at least 4" larger than the quilt top on all sides.

2 Layer the quilt top with batting and backing; baste. Quilt as desired. This quilt was quilted with feathers in the Flying Geese blocks and a variety of quiting designs in the border and large squares.

3 Use the black #4 strips to bind your quilt.

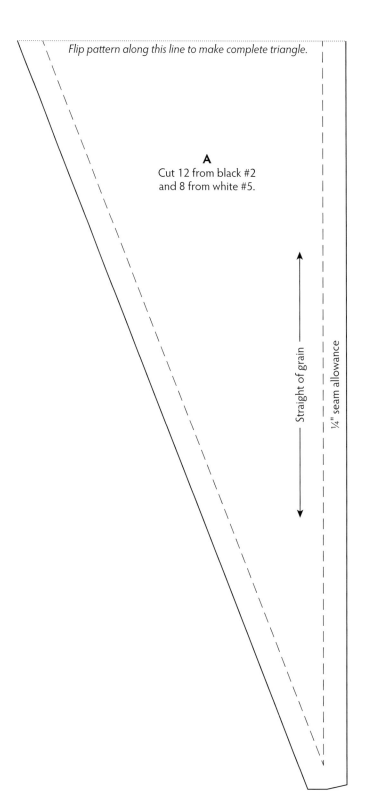

Flip pattern along this line to make complete triangle.

A
Cut 12 from black #2
and 8 from white #5.

Straight of grain

¼" seam allowance

Star Bright

O n my very first date with the man who would become my husband, we spent some time stargazing. We still like to look toward the sky on clear, crisp nights. There is a calming and soothing feeling from seeing the stars twinkling and shimmering so brightly.

Materials

Yardage is based on 42"-wide fabric.

⅞ yard *each* of 16 assorted white prints for blocks

1 yard *each* of dark-red, medium-red, dark-orange, and medium-orange prints for blocks

⅔ yard *each* of dark-yellow, medium-yellow, dark-green, and medium-green prints for blocks

⅜ yard *each* of dark-blue, medium-blue, dark-purple, and medium-purple prints for blocks

1⅜ yards of black print for border and binding

¼ yard *each* of dark-violet and medium-violet prints for blocks

8½ yards of fabric for backing

96" x 96" piece of batting

3½" x 6½" rectangle of template plastic

Add-A-Quarter ruler

Water-soluble fabric glue pen and glue stick

Foundation paper

Cutting

From *each* of the assorted white prints, cut:
1 strip, 6½" x 42"; crosscut into 6 squares, 6½" x 6½" (96 total; 12 will be left over)

3 strips, 6¾" x 42"; crosscut into 14 squares, 6¾" x 6¾" (224 total)

From *each* of the dark-red, medium-red, dark-orange, and medium-orange prints, cut:
11 strips, 2½" x 42" (44 total)

From *each* of the dark-yellow, medium-yellow, dark-green, and medium-green prints, cut:
8 strips, 2½" x 42" (32 total)

From *each* of the dark-blue, medium-blue, dark-purple, and medium-purple prints, cut:
4 strips, 2½" x 42" (16 total)

From *each* of the dark-violet and medium-violet prints, cut:
2 strips, 2½" x 42" (4 total)

From the black print, cut:
9 strips, 2½" x 42"

10 strips, 2¼" x 42"

Cutting the Triangles and Diamonds

1 Layer eight white 6¾" squares, right side facing up and raw edges aligned. Cut the stack of squares into quarters diagonally as shown. Without moving the pieces, cut the squares in half vertically and horizontally to make eight stacks of eight triangles each. Cut all 6¾" squares in this way. Use a large paper clip to hold each stack together. Then place the stacks in a resealable bag.

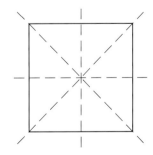 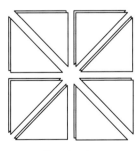

Cut triangles.

"Star Bright," pieced and quilted by Jackie Kunkel

Finished quilt: 88½" x 88½"
Finished block: 6" x 6"

Organizing the Colors

Use resealable bags to keep all the pieces organized. I place each color in its own bag. For example, all the medium reds go in one bag, the dark reds in another bag, and so on. When I've used all the pieces in the bag, I know I've made all the blocks from that color! This is a great way to keep your pieces in order and see your progress at the same time.

2 Lay a dark-red strip on your cutting mat. Position the 45° line of the ruler along the lower cut edge of the strip. Cut along the edge of the ruler to create the angled end of the strip. Then rotate the strip and measure 2½" from the freshly cut edge; cut again to make a diamond. (You can stack your fabric strips and cut through multiple layers if desired. This will make cutting faster, but be careful to be accurate.)

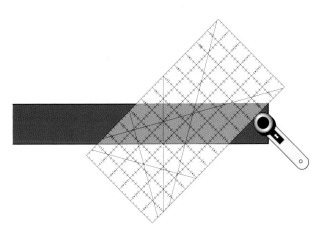

Trim end at 45° angle.

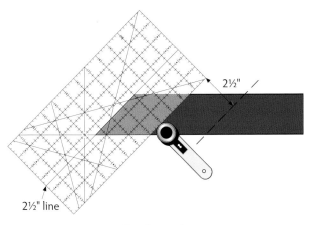

2½"

2½" line

Cut diamonds.

3 Repeat to cut diamonds in the following colors and quantities:

- Dark red and medium red:
104 diamonds of each

- Dark orange and medium orange:
104 diamonds of each

- Dark yellow and medium yellow:
72 diamonds of each

- Dark green and medium green:
72 diamonds of each

- Dark blue and medium blue:
40 diamonds of each

- Dark purple and medium purple:
40 diamonds of each

- Dark violet and medium violet:
16 diamonds of each

Making the Units

1 Make 448 copies each of foundation patterns A and B on page 44. Cut the units apart, leaving about ⅛" of paper all around the outer line.

Preprinted Papers

If you prefer not to make copies of the foundation patterns, you can purchase Judy Niemeyer's Charm Elements Pack #9 at Quiltworx.com. The pack includes cutting templates, instructions, and enough papers to make ten 6" LeMoyne Stars, similar to the one in this quilt. The patterns are printed on foundation paper and provide a stress-free alternative to photocopying or tracing the patterns in this book.

2 Adjust the stitch length to a shorter-than-normal 13 to 16 stitches per inch. This is approximately 1.7 on a sewing machine that has a stitch-length range of 0 to 5. The shorter stitch length makes it easier to remove the paper foundation and makes a stronger seam.

3 To make eight A units, turn one A unit so that the blank (wrong) side of the paper is facing up. With fabric right side up, use a glue stick to glue a dark-red diamond on top of area 1, lining up the edge of the fabric with the edge of the paper. The diamond is oversized and all of the fabric should be on the paper. In the same way, glue dark-red diamonds to the remaining seven A units.

4 Turn the paper and fabric over so that the printed side of the paper is facing up. Place the template-plastic rectangle on the line between areas 1 and 2. Fold the paper back along the plastic to expose the seam allowance. Place the Add-A-Quarter ruler on the fold and use a rotary cutter to trim the excess fabric so that it extends ¼" from the folded line. In the same way, trim the remaining seven A units. *Do not* open the papers; leave them folded.

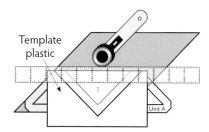

Template plastic

5 Place a white triangle right side up on your cutting mat. Place a unit from step 4 on top of the white triangle, right sides together, aligning the trimmed edge of the dark-red piece with the raw edge of the white triangle. The white triangle should cover area 2. Instead of pins, use a glue pen to dab a little glue inside the seam allowance to hold the pieces together. Prepare the seven remaining units in the same way.

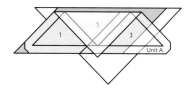

6 Unfold the paper and sew on the line between areas 1 and 2. Chain piece the seven remaining units in the same way. Clip the units apart. Open the fabrics so that both pieces are right side up and press the seam allowances to one side with a dry iron.

Use a Dry Iron!

Steam or water will make your papers shrink. A dry iron is best for pressing the units.

7 Repeat step 4, placing the template-plastic rectangle on the line between areas 1 and 3. Repeat steps 5 and 6, adding a white triangle for area 3. Sew on the line between areas 1 and 3.

8 When the unit is completely covered with fabric pieces, lay the unit on a cutting mat, fabric side down (marked paper foundation up). Use a rotary cutter and ruler to trim the paper and fabric on the outer line. Gently remove the paper. Make a total of 104 dark-red A units.

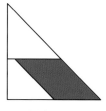

Make 104.

9 Repeat steps 3–8 to make the number of A units as shown.

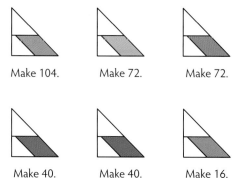

Make 104.   Make 72.   Make 72.

Make 40.   Make 40.   Make 16.

10 For the B units, use a white triangle for area 1 and repeat steps 3–8 to make the number of units as shown.

Make 104.

Make 104.

Make 72.

Make 72.

Make 40.

Make 40.

Make 16.

Making the Blocks

Reset the stitch length to the normal setting, about 2.0 to 2.5 on your sewing machine.

1 Lay out four A units and four B units from one color family as shown. Sew the A and B units together in pairs. Press the seam allowances open to reduce bulk.

2 Sew the pieces together in rows. Press the seam allowances open. Then sew the rows together and press the seam allowances open. Make 26 red blocks.

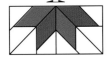
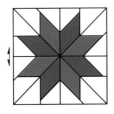
Make 26.

3 Repeat steps 1 and 2 to make the number of blocks indicated for each color combination.

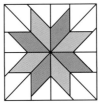
Make 26.

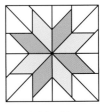
Make 18.

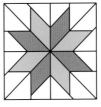
Make 18.

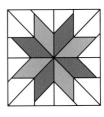
Make 10.

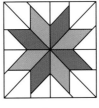
Make 10.

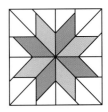
Make 4.

Assembling the Quilt Top

1 On a design wall, lay out the blocks and white 6½" squares in 14 rows as shown in the quilt layout on page 44, making sure each color combination forms a square. Sew the blocks (and white squares) together into rows. Press the seam allowances in opposite directions from row to row. Join the rows and press the seam allowances in one direction.

2 Sew the black 2½"-wide strips together end to end. Measure the length of the quilt top through the center. From the pieced strip, cut two strips to this length and sew them to the sides of the quilt top. Measure the width of the quilt top through the center. From the remaining pieced strip, cut two strips to this length and sew them to the top and bottom of the quilt top to complete the border. Press all seam allowances toward the black border.

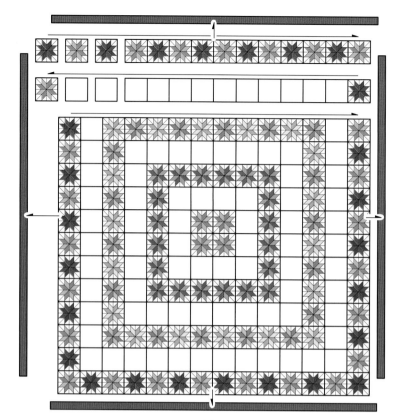

Quilt layout

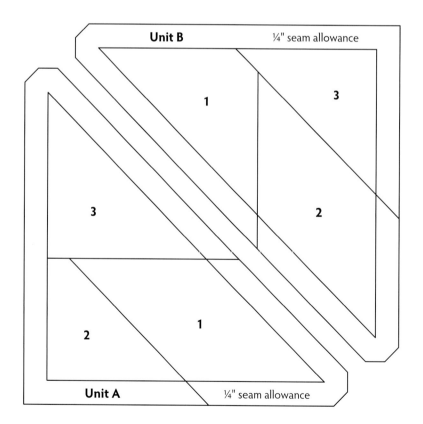

Finishing the Quilt

For more details on any of the following steps, go to ShopMartingale.com/HowtoQuilt for free downloadable information. If you plan to have your quilt professionally machine quilted, check with the long-arm quilter to see how you should prepare your backing.

1 Press the quilt top. Piece the backing fabric so that it's at least 4" larger than the quilt top on all sides.

2 Layer the quilt top with batting and backing; baste. Quilt as desired. I quilted this quilt with an allover feather design.

3 Use the black print 2¼"-wide strips to bind your quilt.

Alternate Version

"Star Bright," pieced by Deb Mella and quilted by Jackie Kunkel. Deb was asked to reverse the values of the fabrics and use black as the primary background. Using solids instead of prints for the brights gives this quilt a contemporary feel.

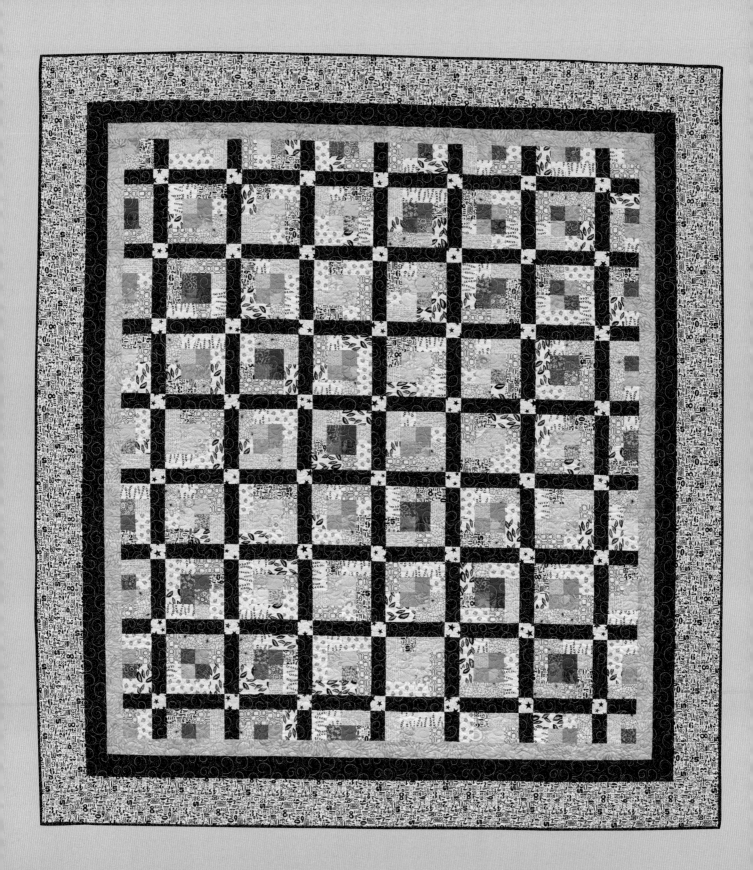

"Hip to Be Square," pieced and quilted by Jackie Kunkel

Finished quilt: 83¼" x 92"
Finished block: 7" x 7"

Hip to Be Square

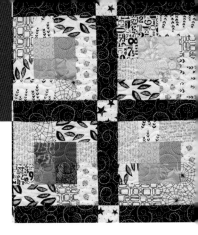

One song I have loved for a long time is "Hip to Be Square" by Huey Lewis and the News. The tune is fun and the lyrics speak the truth, proclaiming: "I know that it's crazy, I know that it's nowhere, But there is no denying it, It's hip to be square!" If you want to be "hip" too, you can make this very square quilt.

Materials

Yardage is based on 42"-wide fabric.

3⅛ yards of black print for sashing, middle border, and binding

½ yard *each* of 6 assorted white prints for blocks

2⅛ yards of white geometric print for blocks and outer border

⅔ yard of teal print for inner border

⅛ yard *each* of 4 assorted orange, red, yellow, green, blue, and purple prints for blocks

⅓ yard of white-with-stars print for cornerstones

8 yards of fabric for backing

91" x 100" piece of batting

Fabric Selection

This quilt is based on color groupings. Each group should consist of four different prints. For the different color groups, I chose mostly medium to dark values and also different prints to give the blocks more interest and movement.

Cutting

From *each* of the assorted white prints, cut:
6 strips, 2¼" x 42"; crosscut into:
32 rectangles, 2¼" x 4" (192 total)
32 squares, 2¼" x 2¼" (192 total)

From the white geometric print, cut:
9 strips, 6¼" x 42"
6 strips, 2¼" x 42"; crosscut into:
32 rectangles, 2¼" x 4"
32 squares, 2¼" x 2¼"

From *each* of the orange prints, cut:
1 strip, 2¼" x 42"; crosscut into 13 squares, 2¼" x 2¼" (52 total; 1 will be left over)

From *each* of the red prints, cut:
1 strip, 2¼" x 42"; crosscut into 7 squares, 2¼" x 2¼" (28 total; 1 will be left over)

From *1* of the yellow prints, cut:
1 strip, 2¼" x 42"; crosscut into 12 squares, 2¼" x 2¼"

From *each* of 2 yellow prints, cut:
1 strip, 2¼" x 42"; crosscut into 11 squares, 2¼" x 2¼" (22 total)

From the remaining yellow print, cut:
1 strip, 2¼" x 42"; crosscut into 10 squares, 2¼" x 2¼"

(Continued on page 48)

(Continued from page 47)

From *each* of the green prints, cut:
1 strip, 2¼" x 42"; crosscut into 9 squares, 2¼" x 2¼" (36 total)

From *each* of the blue prints, cut:
1 strip, 2¼" x 42"; crosscut into 7 squares, 2¼" x 2¼" (28 total)

From *each* of 3 purple prints, cut:
1 strip, 2¼" x 42"; crosscut into 9 squares, 2¼" x 2¼" (27 total)

From the remaining purple print, cut:
1 strip, 2¼" x 42"; crosscut into 11 squares, 2¼" x 2¼"

From the black print, cut:
33 strips, 2¼" x 42"; crosscut *23 of the strips* into:

   97 rectangles, 2¼" x 7½"

   30 rectangles, 2¼" x 4"

8 strips, 3½" x 42"

From the white-with-stars print, cut:
4 strips, 2¼" x 42"; crosscut into 56 squares, 2¼" x 2¼"

From the teal print, cut:
8 strips, 2½" x 42"

Making the Blocks

1 Sew an orange, red, yellow, green, blue, or purple square to a white square to make a two-patch unit. Press the seam allowances toward the darker square. Make a total of 224 units.

Make 224.

2 Sew a white rectangle to each unit from step 1 as shown. Press the seam allowances toward the white rectangle. Make a total of 224 units.

Make 224.

3 Divide the units into six color groups: orange, red, yellow, green, blue, and purple. Lay out four different units from one color group as shown. Sew the units into rows. Press the seam allowances in opposite directions from row to row. Then join the rows to complete the block. Press the seam allowances in one direction. Make 11 orange, 6 red, 9 yellow, 7 green, 5 blue, and 4 purple blocks.

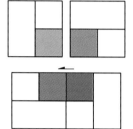 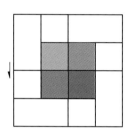

Make 11.

Make 6.　　　Make 9.　　　Make 7.

Make 5.　　　Make 4.

4 Sew together two units from the same color family as shown to make a half block. Press the seam allowances in one direction. Make 3 orange, 1 red, 4 yellow, 4 green, 4 blue, and 10 purple half blocks. You'll have 1 orange, 1 red, and 2 purple units left over for assembling the quilt.

Make 3.　　　Make 1.　　　Make 4.

Make 4.　　　Make 4.　　　Make 10.

Assembling the Quilt Top

1 Referring to the quilt layout at right and beginning in the upper-left corner with the orange unit, arrange the blocks, half-blocks, single units, black sashing rectangles, and white-star squares on a design wall.

2 Sew six blocks, two half blocks, and seven black 2¼" x 7½" sashing rectangles together to make a row. Press the seam allowances toward the sashing rectangles. Make seven block rows.

Make 7.

3 Sew two black 2¼" x 4" sashing rectangles, six black 2¼" x 7½" sashing rectangles, and seven white-star squares together to make a row. Press the seam allowances toward the sashing rectangles. Make eight sashing rows.

Make 8.

4 Sew an orange unit, a purple unit, six half blocks, and seven black 2¼" x 4" sashing rectangles together to make the top row. Sew a purple unit, a red unit, six half blocks, and seven black 2¼" x 4" sashing rectangles together to make the bottom row. Press all seam allowances toward the sashing rectangles.

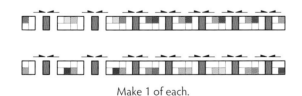

Make 1 of each.

5 Sew the rows from steps 2–4 together. Press the seam allowances toward the sashing rows.

6 Sew the teal strips together end to end. Measure the length of the quilt top through the center. From the pieced strip, cut two strips to this length and sew them to the sides of the quilt top. Press the seam allowances toward the teal border. Measure the width of the quilt top through the center. From the remaining pieced strip, cut two strips to this length and sew them to the top and bottom of the quilt top to complete the inner border.

7 Repeat step 6 using the black 3½"-wide strips for the middle border and the white geometric-print 6¼"-wide strips for the outer border.

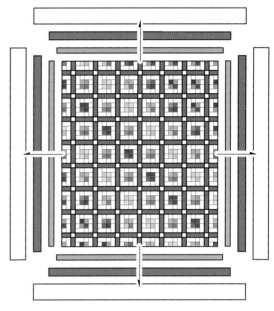

Quilt layout

Finishing the Quilt

For more details on any of the following steps, go to ShopMartingale.com/HowtoQuilt for free downloadable information. If you plan to have your quilt professionally machine quilted, check with the long-arm quilter to see how you should prepare your backing.

1 Press the quilt top. Piece the backing fabric so that it's at least 4" larger than the quilt top on all sides.

2 Layer the quilt top with batting and backing; baste. Quilt as desired. This quilt was quilted with an overall swirl design.

3 Use the black print 2¼"-wide strips to bind your quilt.

Alternate Version

"Hip to Be Square," pieced by Sally Murray and quilted by Jackie Kunkel. Sally was given free rein to use the same block in any setting she liked. She set the blocks on point with sashing and setting triangles. Using purple and pink prints created an entirely hip new quilt!

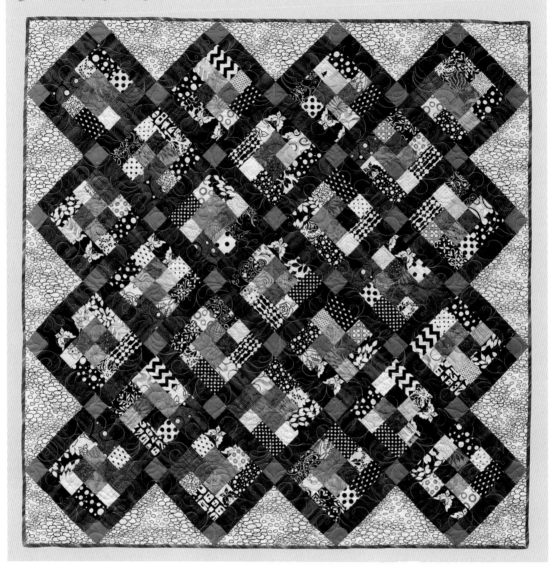

Jumpin' Jax

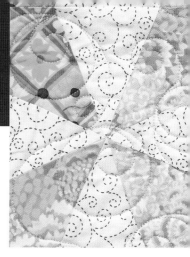

Most of you are familiar with the exercise move the jumping jack, also called the star jump in other countries. This block reminds me of that very movement—hands and legs spread as you jump up and down. What fun and great exercise! So let's all do some "Jumpin' Jax" on the count of three by making this quilt. One, two, three . . . go!

Materials

Yardage is based on 42"-wide fabric.

3 yards of white print for block backgrounds

1⅝ yards of red print for blocks

1⅜ yards of orange print for blocks

1¼ yards of yellow print for blocks

1⅛ yards of green print for blocks

⅞ yard of white-and-black print for border

¾ yard of black print for border and binding

¾ yard of blue print for blocks

⅝ yard of indigo print for blocks

½ yard of violet print for blocks

¼ yard of hot-pink print for blocks

4¼ yards of fabric for backing

73" x 73" piece of batting

3½" x 6½" piece of template plastic

6" x 9" rectangle of template plastic

Add-A-Quarter ruler

Water-soluble fabric glue pen and glue stick

Foundation paper

Cutting

From the white print, cut:
18 strips, 5½" x 42"

From the red print, cut:
9 strips, 5½" x 42"

From the orange print, cut:
8 strips, 5½" x 42"

From the yellow print, cut:
7 strips, 5½" x 42"

From the green print, cut:
6 strips, 5½" x 42"

From the blue print cut:
4 strips, 5½" x 42" (8 total)

From the indigo print, cut:
3 strips, 5½" x 42"

From the violet print, cut:
2 strips, 5½" x 42"

From the hot-pink print, cut:
1 strip, 5½" x 42"

From the white-and-black print, cut:
8 strips, 3" x 42"; crosscut into 16 rectangles, 3" x 13⅝"

From the black print, cut:
2 strips, 3" x 42"; crosscut into 16 squares, 3" x 3"

7 strips, 2¼" x 42"

"Jumpin' Jax," pieced by Jackie Kunkel and quilted by Pamela Burnham

Finished quilt: 65½" x 65½"
Finished block: 7½" x 7½"

Cutting the Pieces

1. Trace the B and C patterns on page 58 onto template plastic. Cut out both templates on the marked lines. The templates are oversized and will make pieces with more than enough fabric for you to position the pieces on your foundation pattern.

2. Using the B template and the red, orange, yellow, green, blue, indigo, violet, and hot-pink strips, trace the number of pieces of each color as listed below. Then cut out the B pieces using a rotary cutter and ruler. After cutting each color, place the pieces in a resealable bag to keep like colors together.

- Red: 60 pieces
- Orange: 52 pieces
- Yellow: 44 pieces
- Green: 36 pieces
- Blue: 28 pieces
- Indigo: 20 pieces
- Violet: 12 pieces
- Hot pink: 4 pieces

 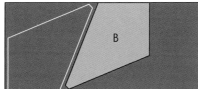

3. Using the C template and the white strips, trace 256 C pieces. Using a rotary cutter and ruler, cut out the C pieces. You can stack your fabric strips and cut through multiple layers if desired.

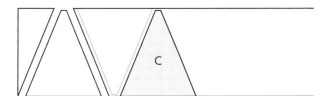

Making the Units

1. Make 128 copies of foundation pattern A on page 57. Cut out the patterns, leaving about ⅛" of paper all around the outer line.

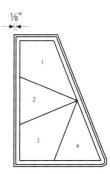

2. Adjust the stitch length to a shorter-than-normal 13 to 16 stitches per inch. This is approximately 1.7 on a sewing machine that has a stitch-length range of 0 to 5.

3. For eight A units, make four stacks as follows: eight red B pieces, eight white C pieces, eight red B pieces, and eight white C pieces. Make one pile by placing the stacks on top of each other and alternating the colors, starting with a stack of white pieces on the bottom and ending with a stack of red pieces on the top.

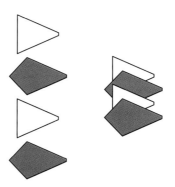

The number-one rule in paper piecing is to stitch the units in numerical order. To speed up the process, I recommend making piles with eight of each piece required to make the unit and chain piecing eight units at a time.

4 Turn an A foundation paper so that the blank (wrong) side of the paper is facing up. With fabric right side up, use a glue stick to glue a red B piece on top of area 1, lining up the edge of the fabric with the edge of the paper. The B piece is oversized and the fabric should completely cover area 1. In the same way, glue red B pieces to seven additional A units.

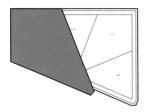

5 Turn the paper and fabric over so that the printed side of the paper is facing up. Place the template-plastic rectangle on the line between pieces 1 and 2. Fold the paper back along the plastic to expose the seam allowance. Place the Add-A-Quarter ruler on the fold and use a rotary cutter to trim the excess fabric so that it extends ¼" from the folded line. In the same way, trim the remaining seven A units. *Do not* open the papers; leave them folded.

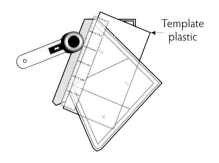

Template plastic

6 Place a white C piece right side up on your cutting mat. Place a unit from step 5 on top of the white piece, right sides together, aligning the trimmed edge of the red piece with the raw edge of the white piece. The white piece should cover area 2. Instead of pins, use a glue pen to dab a little glue inside the seam allowance to hold the pieces together. Prepare the seven remaining units in the same way.

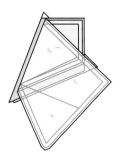

7 Unfold the paper and sew on the line between areas 1 and 2. Chain piece the seven remaining units in the same way. Clip the units apart. Open the fabrics so that both pieces are right side up and press the seam allowances to one side with a dry iron.

8 Repeat step 5, placing the template-plastic rectangle on the line between areas 2 and 3. Repeat steps 6 and 7, adding a red B piece for area 3 and sewing on the line between areas 2 and 3. In the same manner, add a white C piece for area 4 and sew on the line between areas 3 and 4.

9 When the unit is completely covered with fabric pieces, lay the unit on a cutting mat, fabric side down (marked paper foundation up). Use a rotary cutter and ruler to trim the paper and fabric on the outer line. Gently remove the paper. Make a total of 28 red units.

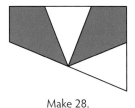

Make 28.

10 Repeat steps 3–9 to make 20 yellow, 12 blue, four violet, 24 orange, 16 green, and eight indigo A units.

Make 20. Make 12. Make 4.

Make 24. Make 16. Make 8.

One Color at a Time

I've found that the best way to tackle these units is by sorting and piecing them in an organized fashion. I like to sew the units by color. I feel a great sense of accomplishment when each resealable bag of pieces is completed.

11 To make the units for the corner blocks, piece four A units *each* as follows:

🡢 Orange B piece for area 1, red B piece for area 3, and white C pieces for areas 2 and 4.

🡢 Green B piece for area 1, yellow B piece for area 3, and white C pieces for areas 2 and 4.

🡢 Indigo B piece for area 1, blue B piece for area 3, and white C pieces for areas 2 and 4.

🡢 Hot-pink B piece for area 1, violet B piece for area 3, and white C pieces for areas 2 and 4.

Make 4 of each.

Making the Blocks

Reset the stitch length to the normal setting, about 2.0 to 2.5 on your sewing machine. Sew the A units together in pairs as shown. Press the seam allowances open to reduce bulk. Make the number of blocks indicated for each color combination.

Make 24. Make 16.

Make 8. Make 4. Make 4.

Make 4. Make 4.

Assembling the Quilt Top

1 On a design wall, lay out the blocks in eight rows of eight blocks each as shown in the quilt layout on page 56, making sure each color combination forms a square. Sew the blocks together into rows. Press the seam allowances in opposite directions from row to row. Join the rows and press the seam allowances in one direction.

2 To make a side border, sew four white-and-black rectangles and three black squares together, starting and ending with a rectangle. Press the seam allowances toward the black squares. Repeat to make a second border strip.

3 To make the top border, sew four white-and-black rectangles and five black squares together, starting and ending with a square. Press the seam allowances toward the black squares. Repeat to make the bottom border.

4 Sew the borders to the sides, and then to the top and bottom of the quilt top. Press the seam allowances toward the border strips.

Finishing the Quilt

For more details on any of the following steps, go to ShopMartingale.com/HowtoQuilt for free downloadable information. If you plan to have your quilt professionally machine quilted, check with the long-arm quilter to see how you should prepare your backing.

1 Press the quilt top. Piece the backing fabric so that it's at least 4" larger than the quilt top on all sides.

2 Layer the quilt top with batting and backing; baste. Quilt as desired. This quilt was quilted with an allover curving design.

3 Use the black print 2¼"-wide strips to bind your quilt.

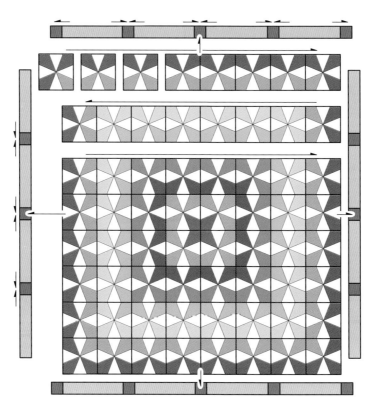

Quilt layout

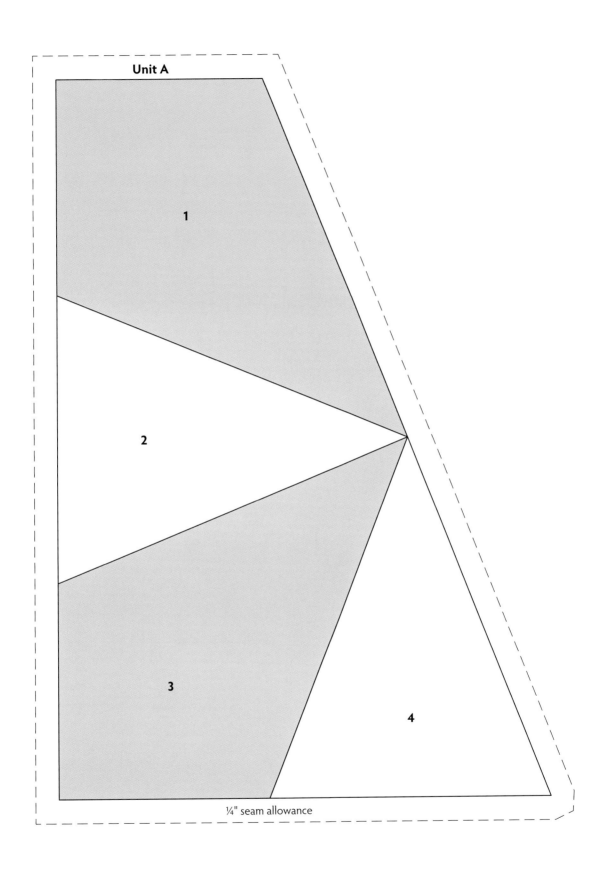

Unit A

1

2

3

4

¼" seam allowance

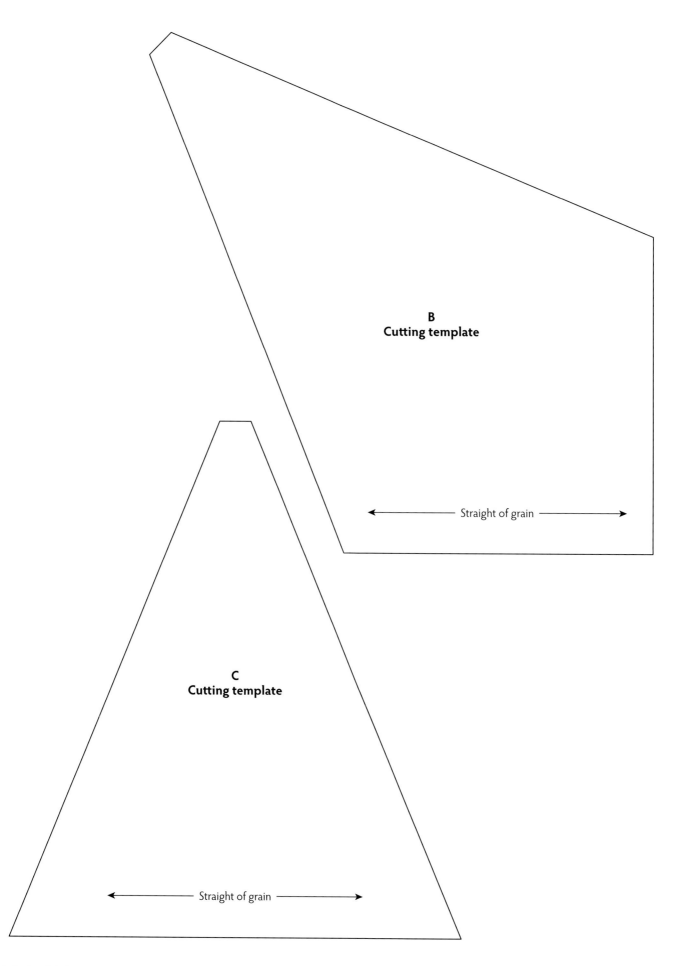

B
Cutting template

Straight of grain

C
Cutting template

Straight of grain

No Snowballs Here

People who know me are well aware that I don't like cold weather, much less snow. Therefore I chose to make my own version of a traditional Snowball block. Actually, it isn't that block at all! Plus, to make it even less snowy, I used African fabrics . . . not much snow there, right?

Materials

Yardage is based on 42"-wide fabric.

1½ yards of multicolored stripe for inner border, outer border, and binding*

¼ yard *each* of 6 assorted white prints for blocks

⅜ yard *each* of purple, blue, and red prints for blocks

¼ yard *each* of turquoise, green, yellow, and orange prints for blocks

⅜ yard *each* of 2 assorted white prints for checkerboard border

⅜ yard *each* of 2 assorted black prints for checkerboard border

4 yards of fabric for backing

69" x 69" piece of batting

*Stripes must run the length of the fabric (parallel to the selvage) to achieve the same results as in the quilt shown.

Cutting

From *each* of the assorted white prints for blocks, cut:
1 strip, 6⅞" x 42"; crosscut into 5 squares, 6⅞" x 6⅞" (30 total; 5 will be left over)

From the purple print, cut:
2 strips, 5⅜" x 42"; crosscut into 10 squares, 5⅜" x 5⅜". Cut the squares in half diagonally to yield 20 triangles.

From *each* of the blue and red prints, cut:
2 strips, 5⅜" x 42"; crosscut into 8 squares, 5⅜" x 5⅜". Cut the squares in half diagonally to yield 16 triangles (32 total).

From *each* of the turquoise, green, yellow, and orange prints, cut:
1 strip, 5⅜" x 42"; crosscut into 6 squares, 5⅜" x 5⅜". Cut the squares in half diagonally to yield 12 triangles (48 total).

From *each* of the assorted white prints for checkerboard border, cut:
4 strips, 2½" x 42" (8 total)

From *each* of the assorted black prints, cut:
4 strips, 2½" x 42" (8 total)

From the multicolored stripe, cut:
5 strips, 2" x 42"

6 strips, 2½" x 42"

7 strips, 2¼" x 42"

Making the Blocks

Separate the colors into groups for ease of piecing the blocks, making sure to use a different white square for each block within the group.

1 Fold a white square in half vertically and horizontally, and lightly crease to mark the center of each side. Fold four purple triangles in half and lightly crease to mark the center of the long side. Stitch triangles to opposite sides of the square, matching the center creases. Press the seam allowances toward the purple triangles.

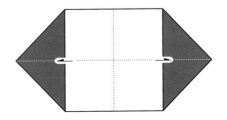

"No Snowballs Here," pieced and quilted by Jackie Kunkel

Finished quilt: 60½" x 60½"
Finished block: 9" x 9"

2 Stitch purple triangles to the remaining sides of the square to complete the block. Press the seam allowances toward the purple triangles. Make a total of five purple blocks.

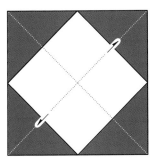

Make 5.

3 Repeat steps 1 and 2 to make four blue, four red, three turquoise, three green, three yellow, and three orange blocks.

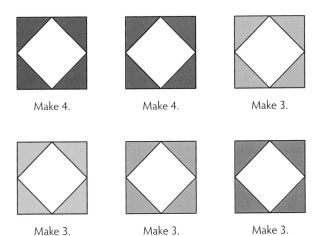

Make 4. Make 4. Make 3.

Make 3. Make 3. Make 3.

Making the Checkerboard Border

1 Pair a white 2½"-wide strip with a black strip. With right sides together, join the strips along their long edges. Press the seam allowances toward the black strip to make strip set A. Make four identical strip sets. Cut the strip sets into 2½"-wide segments, for a total of 52.

Strip set A
Make 4. Cut 52 segments.

2 Repeat step 1 to make strip set B using a different white and black print from strip set A. Make four identical strip sets. Cut the strip sets into 2½"-wide segments, for a total of 52.

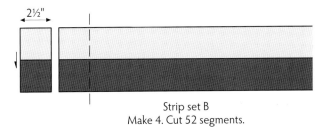

Strip set B
Make 4. Cut 52 segments.

3 Sew an A segment to a B segment as shown to make a four-patch unit. Press the seam allowances to one side. Make 52 units.

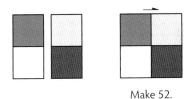

Make 52.

4 Sew 12 four-patch units together to make a side border strip. Press the seam allowances in one direction. Repeat to make a second side border strip. Sew 14 four-patch units together to make the top border strip. Press the seam allowances in one direction. Repeat to make the bottom border strip.

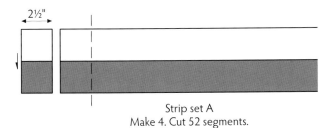

Side borders
Make 2.

Top/bottom borders
Make 2.

Assembling the Quilt Top

1 On a design wall, lay out the blocks in five rows of five blocks each as shown in the quilt layout on page 62. Sew the blocks together into rows. Press the seam allowances in opposite directions from row to row. Join the rows and press the seam allowances in one direction.

2 Sew the multicolored-stripe 2"-wide strips together end to end. Measure the length of the quilt top through the center. From the pieced strip, cut two strips to this length and sew them to the sides of the quilt top. Measure the width of the quilt top through the center. From the remaining pieced strip, cut two strips to this length and sew them to the top and bottom of the quilt top to complete the inner border. Press all seam allowances toward the border.

3 Sew the checkerboard border to the sides first, and then to the top and bottom of the quilt top, making sure to place the same white squares next to the inner border as shown in the quilt layout below and the photo on page 60. Press the seam allowances toward the inner border.

4 Repeat step 2 using the multicolored-stripe 2½"-wide strips to add the outer border.

Finishing the Quilt

For more details on any of the following steps, go to ShopMartingale.com/HowtoQuilt for free downloadable information. If you plan to have your quilt professionally machine quilted, check with the long-arm quilter to see how you should prepare your backing.

1 Press the quilt top. Piece the backing fabric so that it's at least 4" larger than the quilt top on all sides.

2 Layer the quilt top with batting and backing; baste. Quilt as desired. I quilted an allover design of African leaves, which was perfect with the busy fabrics of this quilt.

3 Use the multicolored-stripe 2¼"-wide strips to bind your quilt.

Quilt layout

Alternate Version

"No Snowballs Here," pieced by Fran Adams and quilted by Pamela Burnham. The premise of this version was to again reverse the values. Fran used black prints in the block center and bright tone on tones instead of large-scale prints. Making this a bed-sized quilt is the "biggest" difference. This is an easy quilt to make smaller or larger!

"Dreaming of Pyramids," pieced and quilted by Jackie Kunkel

Finished quilt: 49¼" x 59½"

Dreaming of Pyramids

Oone of the most serene things to see in life is a sleeping baby—so sweet and innocent. As a mother, keeping my kids warm was second nature. When I created this quilt, it was with children in mind. I imagined something bright and cheerful to stimulate their senses while awake and to keep them warm with sweet dreams while sleeping . . . and dreaming of pyramids!

Materials

Yardage is based on 42"-wide fabric.

¼ yard *each* of 8 assorted black prints for large triangles

¼ yard *each* of 8 assorted white prints for small triangles

¼ yard *each* of purple, red, blue, and aqua solids for small triangles

¼ yard *each* of orange, pink, yellow, and lime solids for small triangles and inner border

⅞ yard of multicolored print for outer border

½ yard of black print for binding

3⅜ yards of fabric for backing

57" x 67" piece of batting

Template plastic *OR* 60° triangle ruler

Cutting

From *each* of the assorted black prints, cut:
1 strip, 6½" x 42" (8 total)

From *each* of the assorted white prints, cut:
1 strip, 3½" x 42" (8 total)

From *each* of the purple, red, blue, and aqua solids, cut:
1 strip, 3½" x 42" (4 total)

From *each* of the yellow and lime solids, cut:
2 strips, 2" x 42" (4 total)
1 strip, 3½" x 42" (2 total)

From *each* of the orange and pink solids, cut:
1 strip, 2" x 42" (2 total)
1 strip, 3½" x 42" (2 total)

From the multicolored print, cut:
6 strips, 4½" x 42"

From the black print for binding, cut:
6 strips, 2¼" x 42"

Making the Triangle Units

1 Trace the A, B, C, and D templates on page 69 onto template plastic. Cut out the templates on the marked lines.

2 Position the A and B templates on a black 6½"-wide strip, aligning the top and bottom of the templates with the edges of the strip. Trace five A triangles, one B triangle, and one B reversed triangle on each strip as shown. Use a rotary cutter and ruler to cut out the triangles. Make 40 black A triangles, four black B triangles, and four black B reversed triangles.

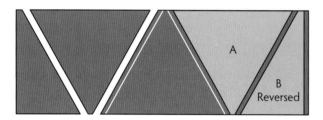

3 In the same way, position the C and D templates on a white strip, aligning the top and bottom of the templates with the edges of the strip. Trace a total of 128 C triangles, four D triangles, and four D reversed triangles onto the white strips. Use a rotary cutter and ruler to cut out the triangles.

4 Position the C and D templates on a solid 3½"-wide strip, aligning the top and bottom of the templates with the edges of the strip. Trace a total of 40 C triangles, four D triangles, and four D reversed triangles onto the solid strips. Use a rotary cutter and ruler to cut out the triangles.

5 On a design wall, lay out the A, B, C, and D triangles in eight rows as shown in the quilt layout on page 67. Rearrange the triangles until you are pleased with the appearance.

6 To make the pieced units, sew white C triangles to opposite sides of a solid-color C triangle as shown. Press the seam allowances open. Sew a white C triangle to the bottom edge to complete the unit. Press the seam allowances

open. Return the unit to the design wall. Make a total of 40 units.

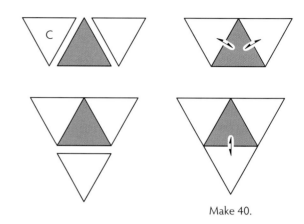

Make 40.

7 To make a half unit, sew a solid-color D triangle to a white C triangle. Press the seam allowances open. Sew a white D reversed triangle to the bottom edge to complete the unit. Make four half units.

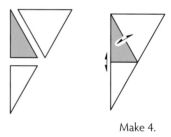

Make 4.

8 To make a reversed half unit, sew a solid-color D reversed triangle to a white C triangle. Press the seam allowances open. Sew a white D triangle to the bottom edge to complete the unit. Make four reversed half units.

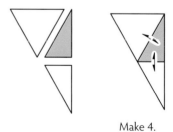

Make 4.

Assembling the Quilt Top

1 Sew the black A and B triangles, pieced units, and half units together in eight rows, referring to the quilt layout diagram at right. Press the seam allowances open. Sew the rows together, matching the seam intersections. Press the seam allowances open.

2 Join the lime 2"-wide strips end to end. Then join the yellow 2"-wide strips end to end. Measure the length of the quilt top through the center. From each of the pieced strips, cut one strip to this length. Sew the lime strip to the left side of the quilt top. Sew the yellow strip to the right side of the quilt top. Press the seam allowances toward the borders. Measure the width of the quilt top through the center. Trim each of the pink and orange 2"-wide strips to this length. Sew the pink strip to the top edge and the orange strip to the bottom edge of the quilt top to complete the inner border. Press the seam allowances toward the borders.

3 Join the multicolored strips end to end. Measure the length of the quilt top through the center. From the pieced strip, cut two strips to this length and sew them to the sides of the quilt top. Measure the width of the quilt top through the center. From the remaining pieced strip, cut two strips to this length and sew them to the top

and bottom of the quilt top to complete the outer border. Press all seam allowances toward the border.

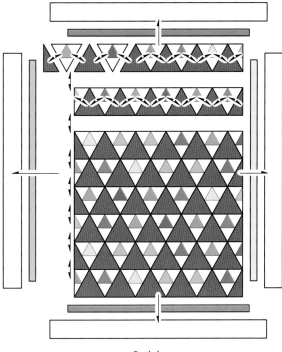

Quilt layout

Finishing the Quilt

For more details on any of the following steps, go to ShopMartingale.com/HowtoQuilt for free downloadable information. If you plan to have your quilt professionally machine quilted, check with the long-arm quilter to see how you should prepare your backing.

1 Press the quilt top. Piece the backing fabric so that it's at least 4" larger than the quilt top on all sides.

2 Layer the quilt top with batting and backing; baste. Quilt as desired. In keeping with all the dots on the fun print, I chose to quilt an allover bubble design on this quilt.

3 Use the black-print 2¼"-wide strips to bind your quilt.

Alternate Version

"Dreaming of Pyramids," pieced by Sally Murray and quilted by Jackie Kunkel. In contrast to my version, Sally used black-and-white prints, similar to some of the other quilts in this book. Using different prints and reversing the placement of the lights and darks, gives the quilt a totally different look and feel.

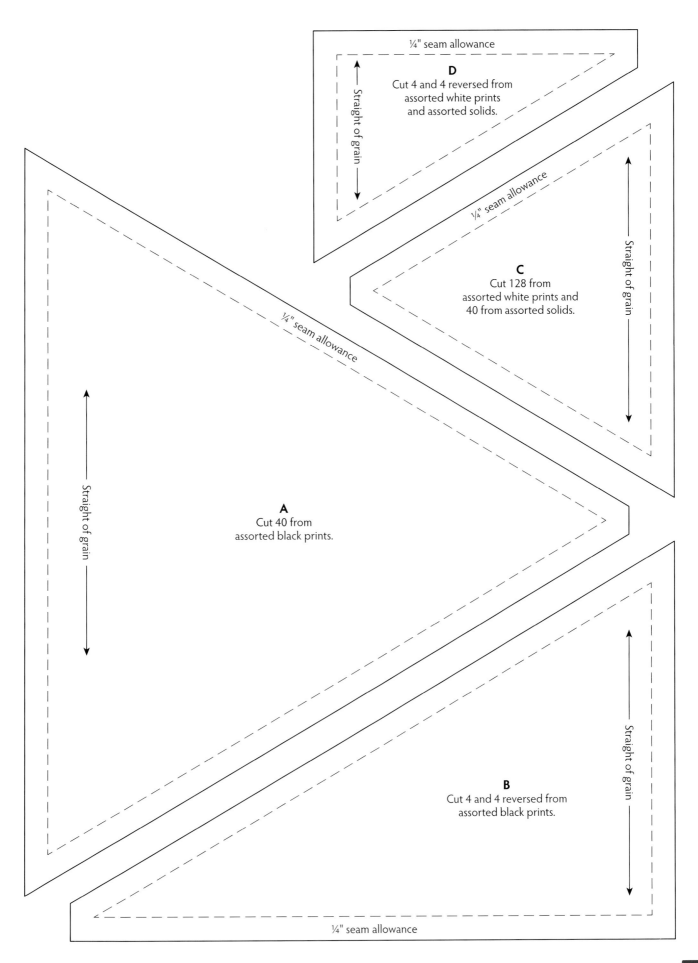

D
Cut 4 and 4 reversed from
assorted white prints
and assorted solids.

¼" seam allowance

Straight of grain

¼" seam allowance

C
Cut 128 from
assorted white prints and
40 from assorted solids.

Straight of grain

¼" seam allowance

Straight of grain

A
Cut 40 from
assorted black prints.

B
Cut 4 and 4 reversed from
assorted black prints.

Straight of grain

¼" seam allowance

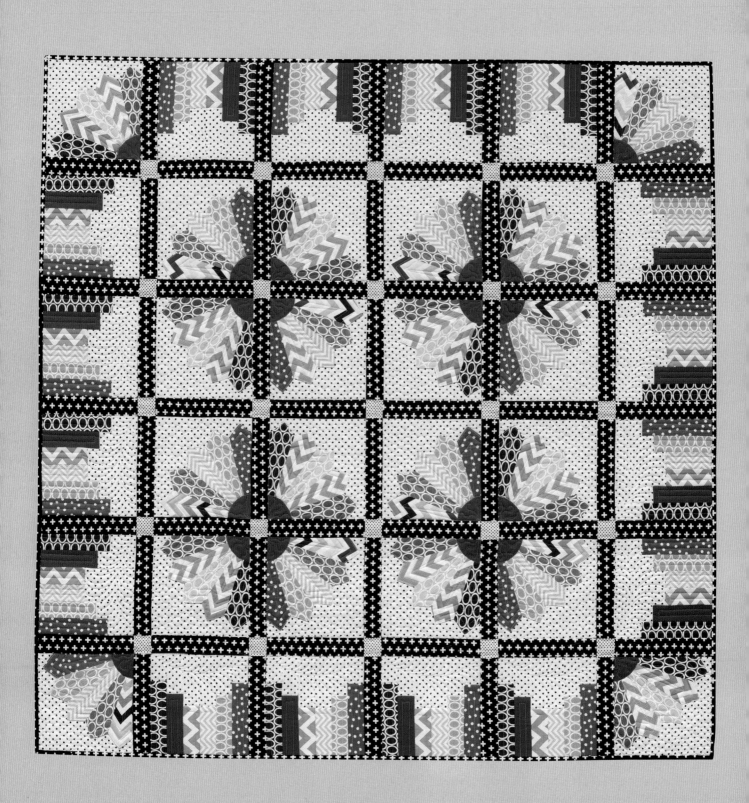

"Twirling," pieced by Jackie Kunkel and quilted by Margaret Solomon Gunn

Finished quilt: 57½" x 57½"
Finished block: 8¼" x 8¼"

Twirling

One of my favorite things to do is dance. From tap and ballet to modern dance, I love it all! My fondest memory is of watching my grandparents move the coffee table aside and dance in the living room together. Waltzing away, they were so happy! Pop-Pop twirled Nana around with ease. These Dresden plates remind me of the two of them twirling around and around.

Materials

Yardage is based on 42"-wide fabric.

½ yard *each* of 2 red, 2 yellow, 2 orange, 2 green, 1 blue, and 1 navy print for blocks

2 yards of large-scale white dot for blocks

1½ yards of black print for sashing and binding

⅓ yard of purple solid for border blocks and quarter circles

¼ yard of small-scale white dot for cornerstones

3⅝ yards of fabric for backing

65" x 65" piece of batting

Template plastic

Water-soluble fabric glue pen

Cutting

From the large-scale white dot, cut:
5 strips, 8¾" x 42"; crosscut into 20 squares, 8¾" x 8¾"

11 strips, 1⅞" x 42"; crosscut into:

32 rectangles, 1⅞" x 4¾"

32 rectangles, 1⅞" x 3¾"

32 rectangles, 1⅞" x 2¾"

From *each* of 1 red, 1 yellow, 1 orange, 1 green, and the blue print, cut:
1 strip, 7" x 42" (5 total)

From *each* of 1 red and the navy print, cut:
3 strips, 1⅞" x 42"; crosscut into 16 rectangles, 1⅞" x 6½" (32 total)

1 strip, 7" x 42" (2 total)

From *each* of 1 yellow and 1 green print, cut:
2 strips, 1⅞" x 42"; crosscut into 16 rectangles, 1⅞" x 4½" (32 total)

1 strip, 7" x 42" (2 total)

From 1 orange print, cut:
3 strips, 1⅞" x 42"; crosscut into 16 rectangles, 1⅞" x 5½"

1 strip, 7" x 42"

From the purple solid, cut:
3 strips, 1⅞" x 42"; crosscut into 16 rectangles, 1⅞" x 5½"

1 strip, 2¼" x 42"

From the small-scale white dot, cut:
2 strips, 2" x 2"; crosscut into 25 squares, 2" x 2"

From the black print, cut:
15 strips, 2" x 42"; crosscut into 60 rectangles, 2" x 8¾"

7 strips, 2¼" x 42"

Making the Dresden Blocks

1 Trace the A and B patterns on page 74 onto template plastic. Cut out both templates on the marked lines.

2 Position the A template on a red strip and trace 10 A shapes. Using a rotary cutter and ruler, cut out the shapes. Repeat to cut 10 A pieces from the other red strip. In the same way, cut 20 yellow, 20 orange, 20 green, 10 blue, and 10 navy A pieces.

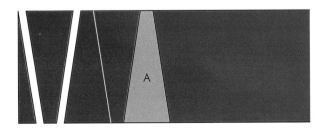

3 Fold an A piece in half lengthwise with right sides together. Sew across the end using a ¼" seam allowance.

4 Turn the piece right side out and use a bluntly pointed object (like a knitting needle or chopstick) to gently push out the tip. Press the blade flat as shown. Make a total of 100 blades.

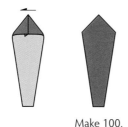

Make 100.

Assembly-Line Style

Chain sew across the ends of all the A pieces. Then turn all the pieces right side out. Finally, press all the pieces.

5 Lay out one blade of each color in the following order: blue, green, yellow, orange, and red. Aligning the shoulders of the blades, sew the blades together using a ¼" seam allowance. Press the seam allowances open. Make 20.

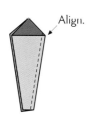
Align.

6 Position the B template on the purple strip and trace 20 B shapes. Use a rotary cutter to cut out the shapes.

7 Using a glue pen, dab glue in the seam allowance of a purple quarter circle. Aligning the straight edges, place a quarter circle on top of a unit from step 5 as shown, making sure to cover the ends of the blades. Make 20.

Make 20.

8 Stitch the quarter circles in place using a blanket or narrow zigzag stitch. Turn the unit over to the wrong side; trim the ends of the blades, leaving a ¼" seam allowance. Make 20.

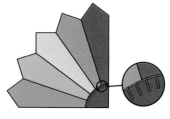

Make 20.

9 Pin a unit from step 7 on top of a white 8¾" square, aligning the straight edges in one corner as shown. Topstitch in place. Make 20 blocks.

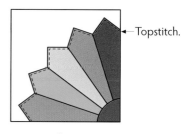

Topstitch.

Make 20.

Raw-Edge Appliqué

There are many ways to appliqué. In this quilt, I used raw-edge appliqué and a blanket stitch for the quarter circles, and I topstitched the blades to the background square. You can easily adapt this block to hand appliqué if you prefer.

10 Turn each block over to the wrong side and trim away the excess white background, leaving a ¼" seam allowance.

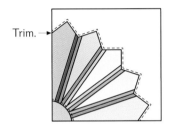

Trim.

Making the Border Blocks

1 Sew a white 1⅞" x 2¾" rectangle to one end of each red and navy rectangle to make a pieced strip. Make 16 of each. Press all seam allowances toward the darker rectangle.

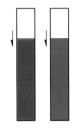

Make 16 of each.

2 Sew a white 1⅞" x 3¾" rectangle to each orange and purple rectangle to make a pieced strip. Make 16 of each. Press all seam allowances toward the darker rectangle.

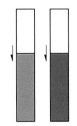

Make 16 of each.

3 Sew a white 1⅞" x 4¾" rectangle to each green and yellow rectangle to make a pieced strip. Make 16 of each. Press all seam allowances toward the darker rectangle.

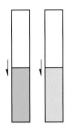

Make 16 of each.

4 Lay out one pieced strip of each color as shown. Sew the strips together. Press the seam allowances in one direction. The block should measure 8¾" x 8¾". Make 16 blocks.

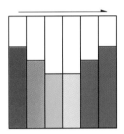

Make 16.

Assembling the Quilt Top

1 On a design wall, lay out the Dresden blocks, border blocks, black sashing rectangles, and white 2" squares in rows as shown in the quilt layout below.

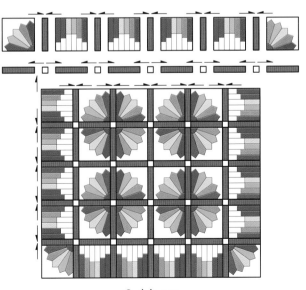

Quilt layout

2 Sew six blocks and five black sashing rectangles together to make a block row. Press the seam allowances toward the sashing rectangles. Make six rows.

3 Sew six black sashing rectangles and five white squares together to make a sashing row. Press the seam allowances toward the sashing rectangles. Make five rows.

4 Sew the block rows and sashing together as shown in the quilt layout. Press the seam allowances toward the sashing rows.

Finishing the Quilt

For more details on any of the following steps, go to ShopMartingale.com/HowtoQuilt for free downloadable information. If you plan to have your quilt professionally machine quilted, check with the long-arm quilter to see how you should prepare your backing.

1 Press the quilt top. Piece the backing fabric so that it's at least 4" larger than the quilt top on all sides.

2 Layer the quilt top with batting and backing; baste. Quilt as desired. Margaret quilted various designs on this quilt. She used feathers in the background and switched thread colors to quilt the sashing and Dresden blocks.

3 Use the black-print 2¼"-wide strips to bind your quilt.

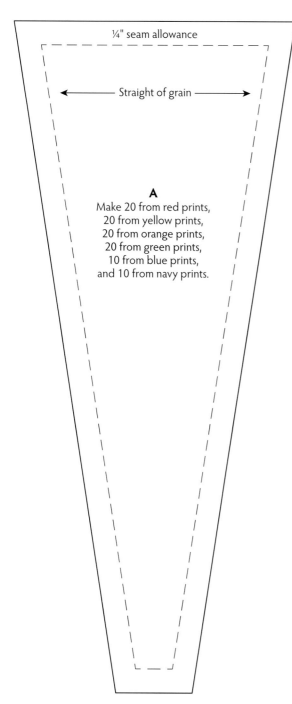

¼" seam allowance

← Straight of grain →

A
Make 20 from red prints,
20 from yellow prints,
20 from orange prints,
20 from green prints,
10 from blue prints,
and 10 from navy prints.

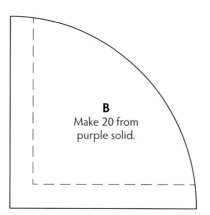

B
Make 20 from
purple solid.

Pattern does not include seam allowance along curved edge. Add ¼" seam allowance for hand appliqué.

Alternate Version

"Twirling," pieced and quilted by Karen Kebinger. Karen used batiks in this version, which creates a more traditional look than the modern fabrics used in the original quilt. The colors of the bright, bold batiks really pop against the black background. Karen also reversed the position of the light and dark values in this version. Also note that Karen chose a slightly different layout for the Dresden blocks.

Tools for Success and Curved Piecing

One of the reminders I always give my students is that there is more than one way to do something. That holds true for making all the quilts in this book. In this section you'll find descriptions of a few tools I recommend, as well as a curved-piecing technique that may be new to you.

Recommended Tools

This section provides an overview of the tools needed to make your quilting projects successful and help you throughout the process.

Thread

For piecing, I use a 50-weight thread. I find that this thinner weight provides more accuracy than a heavier thread and allows quilts to lie much flatter. Also, when making paper foundation projects, the 50-weight thread reduces the bulk that might occur when using a heavier thread such as 40 weight.

Machine Needles

Most quilters typically use a universal needle for their sewing machine while piecing. I prefer using a Microtex Sharp 70/10 (A). This needle has a sharper point and is thinner than a universal needle, and it makes smaller holes in the fabric. Universal needles are more rounded. But remember: the smaller the number, the smaller the size of the needle, which means a 70/10 needle is smaller than an 80/12.

Fabric Glue

There are lots of fabric-glue products available, but these are the two products I use. When gluing fabric to paper, I prefer an UHU Glue Stick (B); it goes on clear and is water-soluble. I use a glue pen when gluing two pieces of fabric together. Fons and Porter's Glue Pen (C) is a water-soluble

fabric glue marker with a narrow shape that allows for very precise application. The glue is blue but the color fades as the glue dries and any remaining glue washes out.

Pins

My favorite pins, hands down, are Clover Fine Quilting Pins (D). They are long with a glass head and extremely thin, characteristics that allow you to weave the pin in place without causing too much distortion.

That Purple Thang

That Purple Thang by Little Foot (E) is actually a multipurpose tool that's available at quilt shops and online. You can use it as a stiletto, as a ¼" guide, and to help sew curves. When sewing curves, use the flat side of the slightly curved tip in front of your needle to distribute any bulk caused by fabric.

Add-A-Quarter Ruler

This specially designed ruler (F) has a lip on it. When paper foundation piecing, place the lip of the ruler against the fold of the foundation paper. Then use a rotary cutter to trim the excess fabric, leaving a ¼" seam allowance.

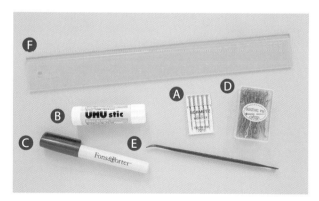

Tools used for the projects in this book

Curved Piecing Technique

I used this technique to piece the curves in "Proud Mary" on page 9 and "Lava Lamps" on page 13. What is nice about this technique is that very minimal pinning is needed. When joining curves, you'll always have a convex side and concave side that need to be sewn together.

1 Place the B piece on top of the A piece, right sides together and matching the straight edges of the B piece with the straight edges of the A piece. Making sure the edges are perfectly aligned, weave a single long, fine pin through both fabrics. Weaving the pins through the fabrics prevents your block from becoming distorted and helps keep it square.

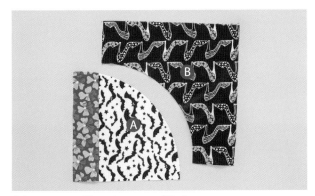

Select convex (A) and concave (B) pieces.

Pin the B piece on top of the A piece.

Use pin weaving on the straight edges.

2 Using a glue pen, start on the right side and dab a little glue inside the seam allowance on the A piece. Press the seam allowance of the B piece onto the glue, matching the raw edges. Continue in the same way until you reach the left side of the curve. When matching the raw edges of the A and B pieces, *do not* pull on the edge of the B piece. The edge is bias and will stretch. Simply place the B piece on top of the A piece without pulling. The edges should match perfectly and there should not be any extra fabric when you reach the left side. The advantage of gluing instead of pinning is that you don't have to worry about hitting pins as you sew. If you make a mistake while gluing, you can easily take the pieces apart, taking care not to stretch the edges.

Dab glue along the curved seam allowance.

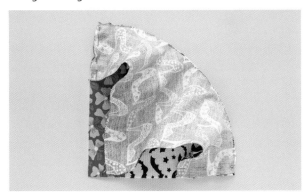

Finger-press curved edges together. You're ready to sew, with edges all matched and even.

3 With the B piece on top and starting on the left edge, sew the pieces together using a ¼" seam allowance. If you have a ¼" patchwork foot, use the edge of the foot as a guide. Use the flat side of the curved tip on That Purple Thang to smooth out any wrinkles in front of the needle as you sew. Press the seam allowances toward the B piece.

Video Tip

You can view a video tutorial featuring the curved piecing technique on my YouTube channel. The link is available on my website: cvquiltworks.com.

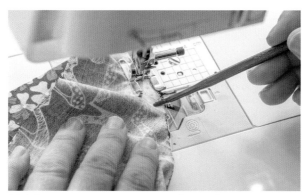

With B piece on top, use ¼" presser foot and That Purple Thang to sew the curve.

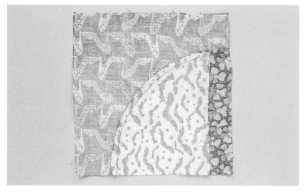

Press the seam allowance toward the B unit.

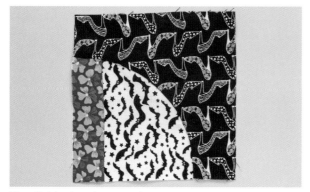

Your finished perfect curve!

Resources

Refer to the listings below to purchase fabric and supplies for making the quilts in this book. Included are manufacturers that supplied tons of the fabric used in the projects.

Online Sources for Fabric and Quilting Supplies

Canton Village Quilt Works
Jackie's Online Quilt Shop and Certified Judy Niemeyer Shop
CVQuiltworks.com

Judy Niemeyer Quilting
Quiltworx.com

Fabric Manufacturers

Clothworks Fabrics
Clothworks.com

Henry Glass & Co. Fabrics
HenryGlassFabrics.com

Robert Kaufman Fabrics
RobertKaufman.com

Timeless Treasures Fabrics
TTFabrics.com

Windham Fabrics
WindhamFabrics.com

Long-Arm Quilting Services

Pamela Burnham of The Quilter's Needle
burnham.pam@gmail.com

Margaret Solomon Gunn of Mainely Quilts of Love
MainelyQuiltsofLove.com
QuiltsofLove.blogspot.com
margaret@mainelyquiltsoflove.com

Acknowledgments

I'd like to extend a few very special thank-yous to some very special friends and family members who helped in more ways than I can count.

🧤 Beside me at every step has been Rod, my ever-supportive husband, who cheered me on, especially when I doubted myself. He is my rock and my guiding light of reason whenever I need it most. Rod, you have my heart.

🧤 Adrianne and Brian, my awesome children who always ask for and love all the quilts I make, and continue to want more.

🧤 My mom and dad, who are always there to cheer for me when I need it. I love you both more than you will ever know.

🧤 Thank you, Karen Burns, for taking that leap of faith.

🧤 One of my best friends, Deb Mella, had my back in more ways than one throughout the entire process. Running Canton Village Quilt Works when I couldn't, she never faltered. I heart you, girlfriend!

🧤 Fran Adams, what can I say? She is a binding and label phenom, not to mention maker of two alternate quilts. The list of tasks Fran took on could fill another book. You are the best.

🧤 Caroline Berman, another bestie, has been there from the get-go. Even with her busy life, she didn't hesitate to make the very first alternate project for "Lava Lamps." She always has my back, and always with a smile.

🧤 Sally Murray is a very good friend whom I met through blogging, and our friendship has progressed from there. She is a dynamo filled with fabulous ideas, and was also quick to help out with three quilts for the book. I hope you know, Sally, that you are Number One on my list.

🧤 Roberta Stoddard is someone I have known for quite a while. Her love of quilting and her generosity are beyond compare, and receiving her offer of help made me happier than I can say. Thank you, Roberta.

🧤 Lisa Slinsky provided help that was so wonderful and timely. She was happy to assist! She's a great friend and sounding board. I heart you, Lisa! Thank you.

🧤 Karen Kebinger jumped in at the last minute without hesitation. She is one of my "newer" quilting buddies, but certainly one of the best. Having her as part of this journey was very important. You rock, Karen!

🧤 David Archambault is the BEST photographer, and had the brilliant skill to make me look, well, 29ish? Thank you.

To two of the best quilters:

🧤 Pamela Burnham, of The Quilter's Needle, is a great quilter, but an even better best friend! She came through for me by quilting beautiful designs on five of the quilts in this book. You are awesome!

🧤 Margaret Solomon Gunn, the award-winning quilter of Mainely Quilts of Love, showed her stuff in four of the quilts in this book. She also came through with flying colors at the drop of a hat. You totally rock!

About the Author

PHOTOGRAPH BY DAVID ARCHAMBAULT

Jackie Kunkel grew up in northern New Jersey, and as a sixth grader she learned to love sewing garments in a home-economics class. The patchwork pillow she made in class is still in her possession. One of Jackie's favorite things at the time was hand embroidery! She would embroider anything and everything with brightly colored threads.

Jackie graduated from college in 1987, married her husband, Rod, in 1989, and worked at a "normal" job. Fast-forward to 1993: she was finishing her master's degree, working full-time, and expecting her first child. At that time, she borrowed a sewing machine and began sewing baby clothes. Her husband thought it would be good to start a hobby so that she wouldn't get bored staying home with the baby.

Begrudgingly, Jackie took a quilting class, which she disliked because of the techniques taught by the instructor. She took a second class from a different instructor, and fell in love with quilting!

In 2000, she started her long-arm quilting business, Canton Village Quilt Works, and quilted for customers for 12 years. Jackie began a quilting blog in 2007, and in 2009 she opened an online quilt shop. Shortly thereafter, she started designing quilts for magazines and fabric companies. Since she loves paper piecing, Jackie became a Judy Niemeyer Certified Instructor, and Canton Village Quilt Works is a Judy Niemeyer Certified Shop. Jackie travels throughout the country teaching, lecturing, and showing quilts. Teaching, designing, and running a quilt shop are her passions!

Please visit Jackie at www.cvquiltworks.com to see what she is doing in the quilting world.